THE FABER BOOK
OF
TWENTIETH CENTURY VERSE

THE FABER BOOK
OF
TWENTIETH CENTURY VERSE

Revised Edition

edited by

JOHN HEATH-STUBBS

and

DAVID WRIGHT

FABER AND FABER
24 Russell Square
London

*First published in mcmliii
by Faber and Faber Limited
24 Russell Square London W.C.1
Second impression mcmlv
Second edition mcmlxv
Printed in Great Britain by
R. MacLehose and Company Limited
The University Press Glasgow
All rights reserved*

821.08
H351f

CONTENTS

INTRODUCTION
   By John Heath-Stubbs   *page* 23

AARONSON, L. *b.* 1894
   Pesci Misti   33
   The Baptism   34

ABERCROMBIE, LASCELLES. 1881–1938
   All Last Night...   36

ABSE, DANNIE. *b.* 1923
   Letter to Alex Comfort   37

ALLISON, DRUMMOND. 1921–1943
   Dedication   39
   My Sister Helen   39
   The Brass Horse   40

AUDEN, W. H. *b.* 1907
   The Letter   42
   From The Sea and the Mirror   43
   Carry her over the Water   43
   Song for St. Cecilia's Day   44
   From In Memory of W. B. Yeats   46
   Atlantis   48

BARKER, GEORGE. *b.* 1913

    From The True Confession of George Barker   51
    Resolution of Dependence   52
    Summer Song   55
    Elegy V   56
    News of The World II   57
    News of The World III   58

BELL, WILLIAM. 1924–1948

    A Young Man's Song   61
    Elegy VIII   62
    Elegy XII   64

BETJEMAN, JOHN. *b.* 1906

    Parliament Hill Fields   67
    Upper Lambourne   68
    Youth and Age on Beaulieu River, Hants.   69

BINYON, LAURENCE. 1869–1943

    Virgil's Farewell to Dante   71

BLACKBURN, THOMAS. *b.* 1916

    Oedipus   73

BLUNDEN, EDMUND. *b.* 1896

    The Midnight Skaters   74
    Report on Experience   74
    Solutions   75
    The Giant Puffball   76

BLUNT, WILFRID SCAWEN. 1840–1922

    A Storm in Summer   78

BRIDGES, ROBERT. 1844–1930
- The Psalm   *page* 79
- Ghosts   81
- Ἐτώσιον ἄχθος ἀρούρης   81

BROOKE, RUPERT. 1887–1915
- The Funeral of Youth: Threnody   82

CAMERON, NORMAN. 1905–1953
- El Aghir   84
- The Firm of Happiness, Limited   85
- Three Love Poems   86

CAMPBELL, ROY. 1902–1957
- Toledo, July 1936   88
- The Sisters   88
- Choosing a Mast   89
- Luis de Camões   91

CARPENTER, MAURICE. *b.* 1911
- To S.T.C. on his 179th Birthday, October 12th, 1951   93

CAUSLEY, CHARLES. *b.* 1917
- A Ballad for Katherine of Aragon   96

CHESTERTON, G. K. 1874–1936
- The Old Song   98
- The Skeleton   100

CLEMO, JACK. b. 1916
   The Burnt Bush   *page* 101

COPPARD, A. E. 1878–1957
   The Unfortunate Miller   103

CRONIN, ANTHONY. b. 1925
   For a Father   105

DAVIDSON, JOHN. 1837–1909
   Thirty Bob a Week   106

DAVIE, DONALD. b. 1922
   On Bertrand Russell's 'Portraits from
      Memory'   110

DAVIES, W. H. 1871–1940
   The Truth   111
   The Sea   111

DE LA MARE, WALTER. 1873–1956
   The Galliass   114
   Napoleon   115
   The Feckless Dinner Party   115

DOUGHTY, C. M. 1843–1926
   Hymn to the Sun   118
   The Gauls sacrifice   119
   A Roman Officer writes   119

DOUGLAS, KEITH. 1920–1944
    Desert Flowers   *page* 121
    The Deceased   121

DURRELL, LAWRENCE. *b.* 1912
    Nemea   123

ELIOT, T. S. *b.* 1888
    La Figlia che piange   124
    Lines for an Old Man   125
    From Little Gidding   125

EMPSON, WILLIAM. *b.* 1906
    To an Old Lady   129
    Aubade   130

FINCH, ANNE. *b.* 1908
    From Essay on Marriage   132

FLECKER, JAMES ELROY. 1884–1915
    Santorin   133
    The Parrot   134

GASCOYNE, DAVID. *b.* 1916
    An Elegy   136
    Orpheus in the Underworld   138
    The Sacred Hearth   139

GIBSON, WILFRID. 1878–1962
    Henry Turnbull   141

GRAHAM, W. S. *b.* 1917

    To my Father   *page* 142
    The Children of Greenock   143
    Listen. Put on Morning   145
    The Name like a River   146

GRAVES, ROBERT. *b.* 1895

    A Love Story   148
    The Laureate   149
    Ulysses   149
    She tells her Love while half Asleep   150
    Down, Wanton, down!   150
    Nature's Lineaments   151
    Lament for Pasiphae   152

GUNN, THOM. *b.* 1929

    Tamer and Hawk   153

HARDY, THOMAS. 1840–1928

    A Church Romance   154
    Lausanne   154
    Tess's Lament   155
    The Convergence of the Twain   157
    I look into my Glass   158

HENNELL, THOMAS. 1903–1945

    Queen Anne's Musicians   159
    Shepherd and Shepherdess   159
    A Mermaiden   160

HEPPENSTALL, RAYNER. *b.* 1911
    Actaeon   *page* 163

HIGGINS, BRIAN. *b.* 1930
    Baedeker for Metaphysicians   164
    The Enticements of Virtue   165
    All Other Men   165

HILL, GEOFFREY. *b.* 1932
    The Turtle Dove   167
    Asmodeus   168

HODGSON, RALPH. 1871–1962
    The House Across the Way   169
    From Flying Scrolls   169

HOUSMAN, A. E. 1859–1936
    In Valleys Green and Still   171
    Oh who is that Young Sinner   172
    Her Strong Enchantments failing 173
    The Welsh Marches   173

HUGHES, TED. *b.* 1930
    The Lake   175

JONES, DAVID. *b.* 1895
    From The Anathemata   176

JOYCE, JAMES. 1882–1941
    The Holy Office   *page* 178

KAVANAGH, PATRICK. *b.* 1905
    Shancoduff   181
    Canal Bank Walk   181
    Is   182
    To Hell with Commonsense   183
    Dear Folks   184
    Lecture Hall   184

KEYES, SIDNEY. 1922–1943
    Holstenwall   186
    The Grail   187

KIPLING, RUDYARD. 1865–1936
    Ford o' Kabul River   188
    The Looking Glass   190
    Gethsemane   192
    Five War Epitaphs   192

KIRKUP, JAMES. *b.* 1923
    A Correct Compassion   194

LARKIN, PHILIP. *b.* 1922
    Ambulances   198

LAWRENCE, D. H. 1885–1930
    The Ship of Death   199

LEE, LAURIE. *b.* 1914
    Milkmaid *page* 204

LEWIS, ALUN. 1915–1944
    To a Comrade in Arms 205

LEWIS, C. DAY. *b.* 1904
    Nearing again the Legendary Isle 206
    Now she is like the White Tree-Rose 207

LEWIS, WYNDHAM. 1884–1957
    The Song of the Militant Romance 208

LOWRY, MALCOLM. 1909–1957
    Delirium in Vera Cruz 214
    After Publication of Under the Volcano 214

MACDIARMID, HUGH. *b.* 1892
    The Two Parents 215
    O Wha's been here afore me, Lass 215
    Scunner 216
    Empty Vessel 216
    British Leftish Poetry, 1930–40 217
    Reflections in a Slum 217

MACDONOGH, PATRICK. 1902–1962
    She walked unaware 220

MACNEICE, LOUIS. 1907–1963
    The Mixer 222
    Charon 222

MASEFIELD, JOHN. *b.* 1878
    Sea-Change 224

MONRO, HAROLD. 1879–1932
- The Terrible Door   *page* 225
- Street Fight   225

MOORE, T. STURGE. 1870–1944
- A Daughter of Admetus   227

MURPHY, RICHARD. *b.* 1927
- Epitaph on a Fir-Tree   228

MUIR, EDWIN. 1887–1959
- The Wayside Station   229
- The Child Dying   230
- Merlin   231

NEWBOLT, HENRY. 1862–1938
- Song   232
- From Generation to Generation   233
- Commemoration   233

NICHOLS, ROBERT. 1893–1944
- Harlots' Catch   235

NICHOLSON, NORMAN. *b.* 1914
- Cleator Moor   237
- Song at Night   238
- Caedmon   239

OWEN, WILFRED. 1893–1918
- Shadwell Stair   241
- Insensibility   241
- Dulce et Decorum est   244

PALMER, HERBERT. 1880–1961
    The Wounded Hawk *page* 245
    Aunt Zillah Speaks 246

PITTER, RUTH. *b.* 1897
    The Military Harpist 247
    The Tigress 248
    The Viper 249
    But for Lust 250

PLOMER, WILLIAM. *b.* 1903
    Mews Flat Mona 251

POTTS, PAUL. *b.* 1911
    For My Father 254
    The Muse to an Unknown Poet 254

POUND, EZRA. *b.* 1885
    The Seafarer 255
    Sestina: Altaforte 258
    Phyllidula 260
    The Faun 260
      From The Pisan Cantos 261
    ('Tudor indeed is gone')
      From The Pisan Cantos 261
    ('What thou lovest well remains')

PRINCE, F. T. *b.* 1912
    The Token 263

RAINE, KATHLEEN. *b.* 1908
    Worry about Money 264

READ, HERBERT. *b.* 1893
> The White Isle of Leuce *page* 265
> Sic et Non 265
> *From* Mutations of the Phoenix 267

RICKWORD, EDGELL. *b.* 1898
> Cosmogony 269
> The Cascade 269

RIDLER, ANNE. *b.* 1912
> Christmas and Common Birth 271
> Now Philippa is gone 272

RODGERS, W. R. *b.* 1911
> Beagles 273
> Carol 273

ROSENBERG, ISAAC. 1890–1918
> The Immortals 275
> The Female God 275

SASSOON, SIEGFRIED. *b.* 1886
> In Barracks 277
> Stand-to: Good Friday Morning 277
> 'Blighters' 278
> Monody on the Demolition of Devonshire House 278
> Early Chronology 279

SEYMOUR-SMITH, MARTIN. *b.* 1928
> He came to visit me 281

SHORT, JOHN. *b.* 1911
    Carol   *page* 282

SISSON, C. H. *b.* 1914
    The Nature of Man   283
    Ightham Woods   283
    Adam and Eve   284
    Cranmer   284

SITWELL, EDITH. *b.* 1887
    Dark Song   286
    The Drum   286
    Heart and Mind   288
    The Coat of Fire   289
    Most Lovely Shade   292
    The Youth with Red-Gold Hair   293

SMITH, STEVIE.
    The Little Boy Lost   294
    The Bereaved Swan   295
    The River God   295
    The Weak Monk   296
    To the Tune of the Coventry Carol   297
    The Heavenly City   298

SMITH, SYDNEY GOODSIR. *b.* 1915
    The Deevil's Waltz   299

SPENCER, BERNARD. 1909–1963
    Boat Poem   302

SPENDER, STEPHEN. *b.* 1909
    Marston   305
    Your Body is Stars   305
    Song   306

SQUIRE, J. C. 1884–1958
　Under　　　　　　　　　　　　　　　　*page* 308

SYMONS, ARTHUR. 1865–1945
　The Absinthe-Drinker　　　　　　　　310
　Nerves　　　　　　　　　　　　　　　310
　The Grey Wolf　　　　　　　　　　　 311

THOMAS, DYLAN. 1914–1953
　Before I knocked and Flesh let enter　 312
　The Hunchback in the Park　　　　　 313
　This Bread I break was once the Oat　 315
　Ears in the Turrets hear　　　　　　　315

THOMAS, EDWARD. 1878–1917
　The Clouds that are so Light　　　　　317
　Tall Nettles　　　　　　　　　　　　 317
　The Sun used to Shine　　　　　　　　318
　The Owl　　　　　　　　　　　　　　319
　Snow　　　　　　　　　　　　　　　 319
　Thaw　　　　　　　　　　　　　　　 320

THOMAS, R. S. *b.* 1913
　The Survivor　　　　　　　　　　　　321

TILLER, TERENCE. *b.* 1916
　Reading a Medal　　　　　　　　　　 323

TOMLINSON, CHARLES. *b.* 1927
　The Chestnut Avenue　　　　　　　　 324

TURNER, W. J. 1889–1946
　Life and Death　　　　　　　　　　　 325

WELLESLEY, DOROTHY. 1889–1956
    As Lambs into the Pen   *page 326*

WATKINS, VERNON. *b.* 1907
The Feather	327
Indolence	328
The Collier	328
The Healing of the Leper	330
Swedenborg's Skull	331

WICKHAM, ANNA. 1884–1947
The Egoist	333
The Fired Pot	333
Meditation at Kew	334
Vanity	335

WILLIAMS, CHARLES. 1886–1945
Mount Badon	336
Taliessin's Song of the Unicorn	338

YEATS, W. B. 1865–1939
Lullaby	340
Long-legged Fly	340
Parting	341
The Lady's Third Song	342
The Circus Animals' Desertion	343
Song from a Play	344
Lapis Lazuli	345

YOUNG, ANDREW. *b.* 1885
    Stay, Spring   *page* 347
    The Scarecrow   347
    The Dead Crab   348
    The Black Rock of Kiltearn   348

ACKNOWLEDGEMENTS   349

INDEX OF FIRST LINES   359

INTRODUCTION

This anthology attempts to represent English verse written since the beginning of the present century, from Thomas Hardy to today. It is easier than it was a generation ago to survey this body of verse with some attempt at impartiality, and to see the very varied styles and preoccupations, which at different times have prevailed among poets, as all contributing to the expression of the common imaginative experience of the age.

It has not been altogether possible to fix consistent chronological limits in deciding which authors should, or should not, be represented in a book of Twentieth Century Verse. Swinburne and George Meredith both survived into the first decade of the twentieth century, but they are obviously and typically Victorian, and have hence been excluded, as has Gerard Manley Hopkins, who died, indeed, some time before the nineteenth century's close. The fact that Hopkins' *Collected Poems* were not published till 1918, and that he was then hailed, rightly or wrongly, as a 'modern' born before his time, need not be considered in an anthology which is concerned with a broad general survey, and not with an examination of 'trends' and 'influences'. We have also excluded certain minor poets—Lionel Johnson, John Gray, Francis Thompson, and 'Michael Field', whose work seems altogether typical of the period of the eighteen-nineties. But one poem of their contemporary, John Davidson, who seems to look more to the future, has been included. Another very typical 'nineties poet, Arthur Symons, is quite fully represented, because he continued to produce good work right down to the 'twenties of our own century, though his style showed no traces of development even remotely analagous to that of his friend, W. B. Yeats. It is such figures as Hardy, Doughty, Blunt, Kipling and Bridges who most clearly represent the passage of the English tradition from the Nineteenth to the Twentieth Century. With these, chronologically speaking, our anthology begins.

It is with the verse of the British Isles that we have been primarily concerned. Certain poets, born in the dominions, who have made their homes in this country, will also be found here; but we have decided, for various reasons, to regard American poetry as outside our scope. To evaluate contemporary American poetry demands a radical shifting of standpoint for the English critic. Its problems, its preoccupations, and even the geographical and historical sources of its imagery, are far removed from those of British poetry—a fact which the identity of language tends rather to obscure.

But here again, absolute consistency has not been attempted. The impact of Ezra Pound, the period of whose sojourn and influence in England coincides with a critical time in the development of our verse, was so great that a general picture of English poetry in the twentieth century would not be complete without him. No apology is needed for the inclusion of T. S. Eliot, since he has been a British subject for many years; nor for the representation of so English a poet as W. H. Auden, even though by poems written almost entirely since his adoption of American citizenship.

Within these limits, the editors have attempted to cast their net as widely as possible, and to include what seemed to them to be the best of every school.

All good anthologies must—and indeed should—display, to some extent, the personal predilections of their compilers. In the case of the present, unanimity between the two editors has frequently proved impossible; there are poets, and also poems, who owe their inclusion here to the insistence of one editor only, in the teeth of protests from his collaborator. And left to himself, either editor would undoubtedly have included poems which he has in fact let drop in deference to the judgment of the other. We have both, however, attempted to keep clear of paths already sufficiently beaten by other anthologists, and in particular to avoid any sort of duplication of Michael Roberts' *Faber Book of Modern Verse*—an anthology compiled on altogether admirable, but quite other, principles than ours.

Nevertheless, it would be an impertinence to place a collection of the present dimensions before the reader, except as an attempt towards some kind of critical evaluation of the epoch which it covers. The easiest way to criticize any anthology is to examine it, and then castigate its compilers on the score of the poems which they have *not* included. We have conscientiously read not only the collected poems of the poets here represented, but those of many others as well. Any glaring omissions will, therefore, probably be intentional.

Exigencies of space have however naturally also played their part. Some poems included in the original edition are now omitted for this reason.

An experience of violence, of which two world wars were merely the symptom, has been central to the period with which we are concerned. The antithesis of style which we find in twentieth-century poetry is not merely a literary-historical one, to be explained in terms of a 'shift in sensibility', still less of a conflict between 'traditionalism' and 'modernism'. (Poets like Housman and Rupert Brooke were actually the last heirs of the Romantic revolt typified by Shelley, while it is to such poets as Eliot and Pound that we owe the rediscovery of tradition). It is really the contrast of Innocence and Experience.

There was, in fact, more than one element in the pastoral mood which dominated, in poetry, so much of the first twenty years of the century. In Hardy it was a reaching back to an organic past, remembered as a concrete reality, but felt as already dead or dying. In A. E. Housman it was a flight to a country-world which was really a personal symbol of lost innocence, in which, by a kind of self-tormenting irony, the shadow of violence is always present. In Walter de la Mare, the shadow in the garden-world is—but it is no more than a shadow—that of metaphysical evil. So much of the poetry of the 'Georgians'—in some degree followers of Housman—fails to make any permanent appeal because these writers strive to realise a symbol of Innocence, while turning their backs on the challenge of experience. Their country-world lacks actuality, and is opposed to an urban reality which remains unexpressed in their poetry. The best of the pastoral poetry of the century is hardly, if at all, 'Georgian' in style. It is represented by the work of Edward Thomas, Edmund Blunden, Thomas Hennell, Andrew Young and R. S. Thomas. It continues to be written after the 'Georgian' style itself has become a period piece. Stemming from Hardy rather than from Housman, it is related to an older English tradition—that of Herrick, Edward Dyer, Barnes and Charles Tennyson-Turner. This classical pastoralism is that of a class of educated, scholarly men, who yet remain, through their occupation or upbringing, sufficiently close to the life of the rural community for the countryside to be a concrete, not merely a fanciful, reality. It is difficult to suppose this tradition can continue in the face of a changing economy, and a changing relation between country and town; but perhaps in some of the poems of John Betjeman we see its further, and surprising, metamorphosis.

The shadow of metaphysical evil is, as I have said, present in Walter de la Mare's work (but more explicitly in his prose stories than in his verse). It is also, more clearly, in Lascelles Abercrombie.[1] The Georgians reacted against the more obvious poeticisms, and archaisms of the late nineteenth-century diction, but these reforms were merely negative. The poets were content to leave unbroken the mould, established by the Romantics of a hundred and more years before. And the language of Romantic poetry is essentially an instrument for the expression of Innocence rather than Experience.

The emphasis on the importance of common diction, natural speech rhythms, and the importation into poetry of the virtues of good prose—due largely to the impulse of Ezra Pound and the Imagists—was hence both inevitable and salutary. Twentieth-century insistence on 'the real language of men', like the similar insistence of Wordsworth and the Lake School at the end of the eighteenth century, was really a re-assertion of the legitimacy of a style made

[1] This element in his work is not, in fact, represented in this anthology. It is developed only in such longish narrative poems as *Ham and Eggs* and *Witchcraft: New Style*. These are, at once, too lengthy for inclusion and too turgid in style to be quite successful as poems.

necessary by the extension of subject matter which the challenge of Experience demanded. But academic critics have since too often written as if this style were the only legitimate poetic language. The style of Milton has been abused and that of Donne exalted, regardless of the fact that these two poets, in their seventeenth-century context, knew exactly what they were about. Milton, assaying the heroic, naturally confined himself to the high style. Donne's *Songs and Sonnets* made no such pretensions (this is not to deny him essential imaginative seriousness) and were consequently pitched in the low style.

In practice, good poets of different generations in the present century have employed different systems of style and diction; and in some cases poets have used a different style in different poems or at different periods of their development. It is time, I think, for us to allow the legitimacy of this, and not to let some limited theory of the language of poetry pre-judge the merits of a poem. The greatest of the poets of this century, W. B. Yeats, perhaps because he was an Irishman, always retained a strong sense of rhetorical decorum. The contrast between his earlier and later poetry is not really between an artificial and a vernacular diction, but between the limitations of the nineteenth-century Romantic style and one which employs all levels of style as occasion and subject demand.

It is impossible to discuss this matter of language without taking into account the work of James Joyce, for it reflects in a single life's achievement, the vicissitudes of English style from the end of the nineteenth century to the 'forties of the twentieth. *The Portrait of an Artist* recalls the aestheticism of Pater and the 'nineties, as *Dubliners* represents the naturalism which succeeded it. Joyce's early poems, in *Chamber Music*, are somewhat analagous to the Georgian manner in their limitations of form and preoccupation with Innocence, while *Pomes Penyeach* approximate to imagism. But it is *Ulysses* and *Finnegans Wake* which really represent the polarity of twentieth-century style. In *Ulysses*, by the various devices of parody, conversational realism, and quasi-scientific objectivity, the emotional and associative properties of language are, as it were, reduced to vanishing point. This point seems to be reached in the chapter of the 'slaying of the suitors' just before Bloom finally falls asleep. But in the subsequent chapter, the famous monologue of Molly Bloom, these emotional and associative properties begin to return. This monologue already anticipates the method of *Finnegans Wake*. In this last work, each word is made to convey the maximum of such emotional and associative overtones. *Finnegans Wake* opens up a linguistic chaos, like the chaos of the mad-scenes of *King Lear*, and the absolute simplicity which is miraculously achieved in its concluding pages, is like the simplicity of the scene of Lear's reconciliation with Cordelia.

The purgative experience of *Ulysses* may be related to Eliot's earlier poetry—such as *The Waste Land*—and to much else of the poetry of the 'twenties and 'thirties. In poetry the 'vanishing point' is perhaps reached in the work of William Empson. The complementary purgative experience of *Finnegans Wake* may be related to the more affirmative *Four Quartets*. But linguistically *Finnegans Wake* is more closely allied to the poetry of George Barker, Dylan Thomas and W. S. Graham. In these three an elaborate, formal and rhetorical style re-established itself in English poetry.

The poetry of Experience, in this century, is dominated by the image of a City. The importance of urban and mechanical imagery in forming the sensibility of the modern writer, and the modern reader, has often been stressed, if not overstressed. But we limit the imaginative scope of our criticism if we interpret these tendencies solely in historical and sociological terms. Futurism is as much a heresy as is romantic archaism. The significance of the image of the City is rather as an organic symbol of the pattern of relationships imposed, for good or ill, on the life of men once they have left the state of innocence. The City is thus organically conceived, above all, in the work of Joyce. The city of Dublin is in some sense the real protagonist of *Ulysses*. And in *Finnegans Wake* it actually becomes personal in the figure of H. C. Earwicker, while Anna Livia, river and mother-goddess, rounds off the picture, and stands essentially for the world of innocence. In the same way, the City of London, with other historical cities seen in it and through it, dominates T. S. Eliot's *Waste Land*. *The Waste Land* is a poem of disintegration. The disintegration is of those values—of human culture, love, religion—which, ideally, the City was established to safeguard. Because of the Dolorous Blow the city of *The Waste Land* no longer fulfils its ordained ends; within it, sterility and lust take the place of human love, while mystery and the sorceries of divination replace religion.

The 'Futuristic' attempt of the American poet, Hart Crane, to create a positive and affirmative city-symbol may also be noted, although it lies outside the scope of the present anthology. To be related also, is the use (independently of each other) by Yeats and by Charles Williams of the image of Byzantium as a symbol of aesthetic and spiritual order transcending or subsuming historical experience.

In the context of such possible interpretations of the City-image we are in a better position to appreciate the work of that group of poets who were, for a time, almost identified in the public mind with 'the modern movement' in English poetry. In the nineteen-thirties, a decade of social misery and political unrest, Auden, Day Lewis, MacNeice and Spender were applying to the disintegrated and perverted earthly city of *The Waste Land*, an imaginative criticism conditioned by immediate political and social ends. This reaction to the contemporary situation was fundamentally a just one. But, when we have said this, we must realize that this poetry was limited, in a way not altogether different from that in which the poetry of the Georgians was limited. Georgianism was limited not only because its authors excluded from it any apprehension of contemporary social and political realities, but also because it lacked any clear metaphysical basis. When, as in the case of de la Mare and Abercrombie, genuine metaphysical intuitions entered into their poetry, their full expression was inhibited by artificial conventions of diction and imagery. The poets of the nineteen-thirties tended to limit themselves to the apprehension of social and political realities to the exclusion, at times, of much else that was imaginatively valid, though in their later work we detect a renewed search for a valid personal metaphysic.

The poets and critics of the nineteen-thirties affirmed the value of being contemporary, of expressing the common experience, and the sensibility of the age. This was necessary and salutary, but no more than a half-truth. For it is equally the case that poets work against the sensibility of their age, and affirm those values which the *zeitgeist* is in danger of neglecting, or even of actively suppressing. It is pre-eminently the values of the human personality which the social, political and economic trends of the twentieth century threaten to submerge.

If this be granted, we may expect to find that it is the theme of personal relationships on which, increasingly, the poets of our century have laid the most stress. For it is against the survival of personal and human values that the odds, in our mass-civilization, seem stacked.

This is indeed particularly the case in the work of many of the poets who have achieved prominence during the last ten years, since the original edition of this anthology was compiled. Another noticeable and in some ways puzzling development has been the repudiation, to a large extent, of the formal adventurousness of the poets of Eliot's and Pound's generation, as well as of the linguistic adventurousness of those of Barker's and Dylan Thomas's. In some quarters this has been taken as a sign that, in the mid-century, modern poetry has entered upon a phase of consolidation; or that, freeing itself from continental and American influences, it has returned, healthily, to a native English tradition. To others, however, there may rather appear to be some danger of its retreating into a complacent provincialism, as in the Georgians' day. Or we may suspect that faced with a situation of ever-increasing complexity, the poets lack the resources or perhaps the will to make the radical response which it would seem to demand. If so, we must trust that if poetry is to retain its relevance, this phase will pass.

JOHN HEATH-STUBBS

L. AARONSON

PESCI MISTI

They set the fish upon the table,
Octopuses, herring, cod,
Fried in the final shapes of death,
The minor effigies of God.

And soon the busy knife and fork,
Divulged each true anatomy,
While taste distinguished each from each,
Fish-individuality.

'Fish to flesh and flesh to fish'
I thought with every zestful swallow:
'What better immortality
Than upright human flesh to hallow?'

But at these thoughts I thought I heard
A flat-eyed small Leviathan,
Tail to his mouth, crisp, brown, and dead,
Whisper: 'With me the world began.

'Twas I who propt the mortar up
While God worked deftly on the ocean.
Water that fills your eyes with death,
Affords my soul its true emotion.

The upright human flesh indeed!
Original in your very blood
Is this bright tail, torpedo-shape . . .
Did God destroy us at the Flood?'

L.
AARON-
SON

Hastily I speared him thrice,
Swallowed his tail and half his side,
Found him the tastiest of the lot.
And rose from table satisfied.

THE BAPTISM

Like the first seed before man's birth,
I felt all possibilities of earth;
And lying snug within my power
Could not decide which dream should brave the hour.

The sun with restless hooves above my tomb
Pawed all the day; then hurried to its Groom,
Neighing: 'The master will not rise.'
Why rise? Who rise? Whose rest holds all surprise!

The moon with delicate fingers drew
The outer soil and thrilled my body through.
Stiff, as with pulleys hauled I stood,
But found my feet were rooted in that mood.

Daylight broke bread. The vultures tore;
And wings were with the sun on heaven's floor.
I bent my body to my feet.
I strained: I cracked: I walked within the heat.

The sun with terrible fury rode.
The moon no longer drew me by her lode.
None heeded. Earth's sharp points
Entered my feet that no sweet dew anoints.

Then felt I dream's first cutting pain,
And knew why newborn grass can thirst for rain.
My dreams took shape; were buds; were flowers,
And bent this way and that in search of powers.

Thus, with men's gait and flower's trust,
I cried to the Groom! 'I walk because I must.
Harness the sun! I *seek* to ride!'
The wind rose. The flowers fell to fruit. I ride!

L. AARONSON

LASCELLES ABERCROMBIE

ALL LAST NIGHT ...

All last night I had quiet
    In a fragrant dream and warm:
She had become my Sabbath,
    And round my neck, her arm.

I knew the warmth in my dreaming;
    The fragrance, I suppose,
Was her hair about me,
    Or else she wore a rose.

Her hair, I think; for likest
    Woodruffe 'twas, when Spring
Loitering down wet woodways
    Treads it sauntering.

No light, nor any speaking;
    Fragrant only and warm.
Enough to know my lodging,
    The white Sabbath of her arm.

DANNIE ABSE

LETTER TO ALEX COMFORT

Alex, perhaps a colour of which neither of us had
   dreamt
may appear in the test-tube with God knows what
   admonition.
Ehrlich certainly was one who broke down the mental
   doors,
yet only after his six hundred and sixth attempt.

Koch also, painfully and with true German
   thoroughness
eliminated the impossible, and proved that too many
   of us
are dying from the same disease. Yet was his green
   dream,
like yours, fired to burn away an ancient distress.

Still I, myself, don't like Germans, but prefer the
   unkempt
voyagers, who, like butterflies drunk with suns,
can only totter crookedly in the dazed air
to reach charmingly their destination, as if by
   accident.

That Greek one then is my hero, who watched the
   bath water
rise above his navel and rushed out naked, 'I found it,
I found it' into the street in all his shining, and
   forgot
that others would only stare at his genitals. What
   laughter!

DANNIE   Or Newton, leaning in Woolsthorpe against the
ABSE   garden wall
         forgot his indigestion and all such trivialities,
         but gaped up at heaven in just surprise, and with
         true gravity, witnessed the vertical apple fall.

         O what a marvellous observation! Who would have
             reckoned
         that such a pedestrian miracle could alter history,
         that henceforward everyone must fall, whatever
         their rank, at thirty-two feet per second, per second?

         You too, I know, have waited for doors to fly open
             and played
         with your cold chemicals and written long letters
         to the Press; listened to the truth afraid and dug deep
         into the wriggling earth for a rainbow, with an
             honest spade.

         But nothing rises. Neither spectres, nor oil, nor love.
         And the old professor must think you mad, Alex, as
             you rehearse
         poems in the laboratory like vows, and curse those
             clever scientists
         who dissect away the wings and the haggard heart
             from the dove.

DRUMMOND ALLISON

DEDICATION

Had there been peace there never had been riven
Asunder my humility and pride,
My greed and patience. Had I not accepted
The gift of sin I never had been shriven.

Had I not met and missed you in the room,
Had I not lost your body and your leisure,
I had not learned I could dispense with love
Like a blind man unhindered by the gloom.

MY SISTER HELEN

(*Born dead*, 1917)

First the artillery groaned beyond the Channel,
The Zep descended in astounded silver,
At Westcliff then at Caterham cold the mornings
And the short afternoons impatient grew.

There was no cache behind that sliding panel
However, not a letter on that salva
The maid brought in: for all Death's courteous
    warnings,
Helen was charged for love she never drew.

Oh! had she come, that year of submarines,
She would have needed no sagacious kings
No hovering angels no enlightened shepherds;
She would have been her own effectual Star.

DRUMMOND ALLISON

Our very tyrants—those unvanquished queens
Race, Class and Custom, whose great sufferings
Are passed to us; before the rampant leopards,
And lilies in whose flags, we prostrate are:

These would have been her ever-helpless prey.
The mystery of grave doubt with definition
Would have been hers, of faith with toleration;
Her brothers' conquerors all her prisoners been.

March and Montgomery have moved on to-day
Towards the accurate heart and single nation.
Had she been here, our timorous pale elation
Would have flung taller figures on the screen
Of truth and of accompanying contrition;
She would have comprehended
I am at last reminded,
What we have only seen.

THE BRASS HORSE

Never presume that in this marble stable
Furnished with imitation stalactites,
Withheld from any manger and unable
To stamp impatient hooves or show the whites
Of eyes whose lids are fixed, on sulky nights
He asks himself no questions, has no doubt
What he a brazen engine is about.

Diving on some dry region when his rider
Twiddled the key in his untwitching ear,
Forced through his Himalyan paces, glider
Over the Gobi and the flat Pamir,

Trained by telepathy to disappear
And grow from nothing, he was well aware
Of exploitation and unloving care.

Do you suppose he had no means of knowing
The talking falcon and physician sword
That splinters all chainmail, the mirror showing
What slaughter is in store what golden hoard?
Nor as he automatically pawed
And snorted fire in the loud palace yard
Resented the wide-gaping mob's regard?

We cannot guess what thoughts of combination
With the decaying cayman on the wall
Or the snow leopard blinded by elation
Trouble him in his brahmin-carven stall,
For what Arabian mares and ribboned manes
He writhes his motionless metallic reins.

DRUM-
MOND
ALLISON

THE LETTER

From the very first coming down
Into a new valley with a frown
Because of the sun and a lost way,
You certainly remained: to-day
I, crouching behind a sheep-pen, heard
Travel across a sudden bird,
Cry out against the storm, and found
The year's arc a completed round
And love's worn circuit re-begun,
Endless with no dissenting turn.
Shall see, shall pass, as we have seen
The swallow on the tile, spring's green
Preliminary shiver, passed
A solitary truck, the last
Of shunting in the Autumn. But now,
To interrupt the homely brow,
Thought warmed to evening through and through,
Your letter comes, speaking as you,
Speaking of much but not to come.

Nor speech is close nor fingers numb
If love not seldom has received
An unjust answer, was deceived.
I, decent with the seasons, move,
Different or with a different love,
Nor question overmuch the nod,
The stone smile of this country god
That never was more reticent,
Always afraid to say more than it meant.

From THE SEA AND THE MIRROR   W. H. AUDEN

Master and Boatswain

At Dirty Dick's and Sloppy Joe's
    We drank our liquor straight,
Some went upstairs with Margery,
    And some, alas, with Kate;
And two by two like cat and mouse
The homeless played at keeping house.

There Wealthy Meg, the Sailor's Friend,
    And Marion, cow-eyed,
Opened their arms to me but I
    Refused to step inside;
I was not looking for a cage
In which to mope in my old age.

The nightingales are sobbing in
    The orchards of our mothers,
And hearts that we broke long ago
    Have long been breaking others;
Tears are round, the sea is deep:
Roll them overboard and sleep.

CARRY HER OVER THE WATER

Carry her over the water,
    And set her down under the tree,
Where the culvers white all day and all night,
    And the winds from every quarter
Sing agreeably, agreeably, agreeably of love.

W. H. AUDEN

Put a gold ring on her finger,
    And press her close to your heart,
While the fish in the lake their snapshots take,
    And the frog, that sanguine singer,
Sings agreeably, agreeably, agreeably of love.

The streets shall all flock to your marriage,
    The houses turn round to look,
The tables and chairs say suitable prayers,
    And the horses drawing your carriage
Sing agreeably, agreeably, agreeably of love.

SONG FOR ST. CECILIA'S DAY

I

In a garden shady this holy lady
With reverent cadence and subtle psalm,
Like a black swan as death came on
Poured forth her song in perfect calm:
And by ocean's margin this innocent virgin
Constructed an organ to enlarge her prayer,
And notes tremendous from her great engine
Thundered out on the Roman air.

Blonde Aphrodite rose up excited,
Moved to delight by the melody,
White as an orchid she rode quite naked
In an oyster shell on top of the sea;
At sounds so entrancing the angels dancing
Came out of their trance into time again,
And around the wicked in Hell's abysses
The huge flame flickered and eased their pain.

Blessed Cecilia, appear in visions
To all musicians, appear and inspire:
Translated Daughter, come down and startle
Composing mortals with immortal fire.

W. H.
AUDEN

II

I cannot grow;
I have no shadow
To run away from,
I only play.

I cannot err;
There is no creature
Whom I belong to,
Whom I could wrong.

I am defeat
When it knows it
Can now do nothing
By suffering.

All you lived through,
Dancing because you
No longer need it
For any deed.

I shall never be
Different. Love me.

III

O ear whose creatures cannot wish to fall,
O calm spaces unafraid of weight,
Where Sorrow is herself, forgetting all
The gaucheness of her adolescent state,

45

W. H. AUDEN

Where Hope within the altogether strange
From every outworn image is released,
And Dread born whole and normal like a beast
Into a world of truths that never change:
Restore our fallen day; O re-arrange.

O dear white children casual as birds,
Playing among the ruined languages,
So small beside their large confusion words,
So gay against the greater silences
Of dreadful things you did: O hang the head,
Impetuous child with the tremendous brain,
O weep, child, weep, O weep away the stain,
Lost innocence who wished your lover dead,
Weep for the lives your wishes never led.

O cry created as the bow of sin
Is drawn across our trembling violin.
O weep, child, weep, O weep away the stain.
O law drummed out by hearts against the still
Long winter of our intellectual will.
That what has been may never be again,
O flute that throbs with the thanksgiving breath
Of convalescents on the shores of death.
O bless the freedom that you never chose.
O trumpets that unguarded children blow
About the fortress of their inner foe.
O wear your tribulation like a rose.

From IN MEMORY OF W. B. YEATS

Earth, receive an honoured guest;
William Yeats is laid to rest:
Let the Irish vessel lie
Emptied of its poetry.

W. H. AUDEN

Time that is intolerant
Of the brave and innocent,
And indifferent in a week
To a beautiful physique,

Worships language and forgives
Everyone by whom it lives;
Pardons cowardice, conceit,
Lays its honours at their feet.

Time that with this strange excuse
Pardoned Kipling and his views,
And will pardon Paul Claudel,
Pardons him for writing well.

In the nightmare of the dark
All the dogs of Europe bark,
And the living nations wait,
Each sequestered in its hate;

Intellectual disgrace
Stares from every human face,
And the seas of pity lie
Locked and frozen in each eye.

Follow, poet, follow right
To the bottom of the night,
With your unconstraining voice
Still persuade us to rejoice;

With the farming of a verse
Make a vineyard of the curse,
Sing of human unsuccess
In a rapture of distress;

**W. H.
AUDEN**

In the deserts of the heart
Let the healing fountain start,
In the prison of his days
Teach the free man how to praise.

ATLANTIS

Being set on the idea
    Of getting to Atlantis,
You have discovered of course
    Only the Ship of Fools is
Making the voyage this year,
As gales of abnormal force
    Are predicted, and that you
    Must therefore be ready to
Behave absurdly enough
    To pass for one of The Boys,
At least appearing to love
    Hard liquor, horseplay and noise.

Should storms, as may well happen,
    Drive you to anchor a week
In some old harbour-city
    Of Ionia, then speak
With her witty scholars, men
Who have proved there cannot be
    Such a place as Atlantis:
    Learn their logic, but notice
How its subtlety betrays
    Their enormous simple grief;
Thus they shall teach you the ways
    To doubt that you may believe.

W. H.
AUDEN

If later, you run aground
    Among the headlands of Thrace,
Where with torches all night long
    A naked barbaric race
Leaps frenziedly to the sound
Of conch and dissonant gong;
    On that stony savage shore
    Strip off your clothes and dance, for
Unless you are capable
    Of forgetting completely
About Atlantis, you will
    Never finish your journey.

Again, should you come to gay
    Carthage or Corinth, take part
In their endless gaiety;
    And if in some bar a tart,
As she strokes your hair, should say
'This is Atlantis, dearie,'
    Listen with attentiveness
    To her life-story: unless
You become acquainted now
    With each refuge that tries to
Counterfeit Atlantis, how
    Will you recognize the true?

Assuming you beach at last
    Near Atlantis, and begin
The terrible trek inland
    Through squalid woods and frozen
Tundras where all are soon lost;
If, forsaken then, you stand,
    Dismissal everywhere,
    Stone and snow, silence and air,

W. H. AUDEN

O remember the great dead
    And honour the fate you are,
Travelling and tormented,
    Dialectic and bizarre.

Stagger onward rejoicing;
    And even then if, perhaps
Having actually got
    To the last col, you collapse
With all Atlantis shining
Below you yet you cannot
    Descend, you should still be proud
Just to peep at Atlantis,
    In a poetic vision:
Give thanks and lie down in peace,
    Having seen your salvation.

All the little household gods
    Have started crying, but say
Goodbye now, and put to sea.
    Farewell, my dear, farewell: may
Hermes, master of the roads
And the four dwarf Kabiri,
    Protect and serve you always;
    And may the Ancient of Days
Provide for all you must do
    His invisible guidance,
Lifting up, dear, upon you
    The light of His countenance.

GEORGE BARKER

From THE TRUE CONFESSION OF GEORGE BARKER

I sent a letter to my love
    In an envelope of stone,
And in between the letters ran
A crying torrent that began
To grow till it was bigger than
Nyanza or the heart of man.
I sent a letter to my love
    In an envelope of stone.

I sent a present to my love
    In a black bordered box
A clock that beats a time of tears
As the stricken midnight nears
And my love weeps as she hears
The armageddon of the years.
I sent my love the present
    In a black bordered box.

I sent a liar to my love
    With his hands full of roses
But she shook her yellow and curled
Curled and yellow hair and cried
The rose is dead of all the world
Since my only love has lied.
I sent a liar to my love
    With roses in his hands.

GEORGE BARKER

I sent a daughter to my love
    In a painted cradle.
She took her up at her left breast
And rocked her to a mothered rest
Singing a song that what is best
Loves and loves and forgets the rest.
I sent a daughter to my love
    In a painted cradle.

I sent a letter to my love
    On a sheet of stone.
She looked down and as she read
She shook her yellow hair and said
Now he sleeps alone instead
Of many a lie in many a bed.
I sent a letter to my love
    On a sheet of stone.

RESOLUTION OF DEPENDENCE

We poets in our youth begin in gladness
But thereof come in the end despondency and madness.
    (WORDSWORTH: *Resolution and Independence*)

I encountered the crowd returning from amusements,
The Bournemouth Pavilion, or the marvellous
    gardens,
The Palace of Solace, the Empyrean Cinema: and
    saw
William Wordsworth was once, tawdrily conspicuous,
Obviously emulating the old man of the mountain-
    moor,
Traipsing along on the outskirts of the noisy crowd.

GEORGE BARKER

Remarkable I reflected that after all it is him.
The layers of time falling continually on Grasmere
    Churchyard,
The accumulation of year and year like calendar,
The acute superstition that Wordsworth is after all
    dead,
Should have succeeded in keeping him quiet and
    cold.
I resent the resurrection when I feel the updraft of
    fear.

But approaching me with a watch in his hand, he
    said:
'I fear you are early; I expected a man; I see
That already your private rebellion has been quelled.
Where are the violent gestures of the individualist?
I observe the absence of the erratic, the strange;
Where is the tulip, the rose, or the bird in hand?'

I had the heart to relate the loss of my charms,
The paradise pets I kept in my pocket, the bird,
The tulip trumpet, the penis water pistol;
I had the heart to have mourned them, but no word.
'I have done little reading,' I murmured, 'I have
Most of the time been trying to find an equation.'

He glanced over my shoulder at the evening
    promenade.
The passing people, like Saint Vitus, averted their
    eyes:
I saw his eyes like a bent pin searching for eyes
To grip and catch. 'It is a species', he said,
'I feel I can hardly cope with—it is ghosts,
Trailing, like snails, an excrement of blood.

GEORGE 'I have passed my hand like a postman's into them;
BARKER The information I dropped in at once dropped out.'
  'No,' I answered, 'they received your bouquet of
    daffodils,
  They speak of your feeling for Nature even now.'
  He glanced at his watch. I admired a face.
  The town clock chimed like a cat in a well.

  'Since the private rebellion, the personal turn,
  Leads down to the river with the dead cat and dead
    dog,
  Since the single act of protest like a foggy film
  Looks like women bathing, the Irish Lakes, or Saint
    Vitus,
  Susceptible of innumerable interpretations,
  I can only advise a suicide or a resolution.'

  'I can resolve,' I answered, 'if you can absolve.
  Relieve me of my absurd and abysmal past.'
  'I cannot relieve or absolve—the only absolution
  Is final resolution to fix on the facts.
  I mean more and less than Birth and Death; I also
    mean
  The mechanical paraphernalia in between.

  'Not you and not him, not me, but all of them.
  It is the conspiracy of five hundred million
  To keep alive and kick. This is the resolution,
  To keep us alive and kicking with strength or joy.
  The past's absolution is the present's resolution.
  The equation is the interdependence of parts.'

SUMMER SONG

GEORGE BARKER

I looked into my heart to write
    And found a desert there.
But when I looked again I heard
Howling and proud in every word
    The hyena despair.

Great summer sun, great summer sun,
    All loss burns in trophies;
And in the cold sheet of the sky
Lifelong the fishlipped lovers lie
    Kissing catastrophes.

O loving garden where I lay
    When under the breasted tree
My son stood up behind my eyes
And groaned: Remember that the price
    Is vinegar for me.

Great summer sun, great summer sun,
    Turn back to the designer:
I would not be the one to start
The breaking day and the breaking heart
    For all the grief in China.

My one, my one, my only love,
    Hide, hide your face in a leaf,
And let the hot tear falling burn
The stupid heart that will not learn
    The everywhere of grief.

Great summer sun, great summer sun,
    Turn back to the never-never
Cloud-cuckoo, happy, far-off land
Where all the love is true love, and
    True love goes on for ever.

GEORGE BARKER

ELEGY V

These errors loved no less than the saint loves arrows
Repeat, Love has left the world. He is not here.
O God, like Love revealing yourself in absence
So that, though farther than stars, like Love that sorrows
In separation, the desire in the heart of hearts
To come home to you makes you most manifest.
The booming zero spins as his halo where
Ashes of pride on all the tongues of sense
Crown us with negatives. O deal us in our deserts
The crumb of falling vanity. It is eucharist.

Everyone walking everywhere goes in a glow
Of geometrical progression, all meteors, in praise:
Hosannas on the tongues of the dumb shall raise
Roads for the gangs in chains to return to
God. They go hugging the traumas like halleluias
To the bodies that earn this beatitude. The Seven
Seas they crowd like the great sailing clippers,
Those homing migrants that, with their swallow-like sails set,
Swayed forward along the loneliness that opposed,
For nothing more than a meeting in heaven.

Therefore all things, in all three tenses,
Alone like the statue in an alcove of love,
Moving in obedient machinery, sleeping
Happy in impossible achievements, keeping
Close to each other because the night is dark;
The great man dreaming on the stones of circumstances,
The small wringing hands because rocks will not move:

The beast in its red kingdom, the star in its arc:
O all things, therefore, in shapes or in senses,
Know that they exist in the kiss of his Love.

Incubus. Anaesthetist with glory in a bag,
Foreman with a sweatbox and a whip. Asphyxiator
Of the ecstatic. Sergeant with a grudge
Against the lost lovers in the park of creation,
Fiend behind the fiend behind the fiend behind the
Friend. Mastodon with mastery, monster with an
    ache
At the tooth of the ego, the dead drunk judge:
Wheresoever Thou art our agony will find Thee
Enthroned on the darkest altar of our heartbreak
Perfect. Beast, brute, bastard. O dog my God!

NEWS OF THE WORLD II

In the first year of the last disgrace
    Peace, turning her face away,
Coughing in laurelled fires, weeping,
    Drags out from her hatcheted heart
    The sunset axe of the day.

And leaning up against the red sky
    She mourns over evening cities:
The milky morning springs from her mothering
        breast
    Half choked with happy memories
    And fulfilment of miseries.

'I am the wife of the workman world
    With an apron full of children—
And happy, happy any hovel was
    With my helping hand under his gifted head
    And for my sleep his shoulder.

GEORGE 'I wish that the crestfallen stars would fall
BARKER   Out of his drunken eye and strike
     My children cold. I wish the big sea
        Would pity them, and pity me,
        And smother us all alike.

'Bitter sun, bitter sun, put out your lions
    As I have put out my hope.
For he will take them in his clever hand
And teach them how to dismember love
    Just as though it was Europe.

'O washing-board Time, my hands are sore
    And the backs of the angels ache.
For the redhanded husband has abandoned me
To drag his coat in front of his pride,
    And I know my heart will break.'

In the first year of the last disgrace
    Peace, turning her face away,
Coughing in fire and laurels, weeping,
    Bared again her butchered heart
    To the sunrise axe of the day.

NEWS OF THE WORLD III

Let her lie naked here, my hand resting
Light on her broken breast, the sleeping world
Given into our far from careful keeping,
Terrestrial daughter of a disaster of waters
No master honours. Let her lie to-night
Attended by those visions of bright swords
That never defended but ended life.
My emerald trembler, my sky skipping scullion,

GEORGE BARKER

See, now, your sister, dipping into the horizon,
Leaves us in darkness; you, nude, and I
Seeking to loose what the day retrieves,
An immoderation of love. Bend your arm
Under my generation of heads. The seas enfold
My sleepless eye and save it weeping
For the dishonoured star. I hear your grave
Nocturnal lamentation, where, abandoned, far,
You, like Arabia in her tent, mourn through an
    evening
Of wildernesses. O what are you grieving for?
From the tiara'd palaces of the Andes
And the last Asiatic terraces, I see
The wringing of the hands of all of the world,
I hear your long lingering of disillusion.
Favour the viper, heaven, with one vision
That it may see what is lost. The crime is blended
With the time and the cause. But at your
Guilty and golden bosom, O daughter of laws,
I happy lie to-night, the fingering zephyr
Light and unlikely as a kiss. The shades creep
Out of their holes and graves for a last
Long look at your bare empire as it rolls
Its derelict glory away into darkness. Turn, liar,
Back. Our fate is in your face. Whom do you love
But those whom you doom to the happy disgrace
Of adoring you with degradations? I garb my wife,
The wide world of a bride, in devastations.
She has curled up in my hand, and, like a moth,
Died a legend of splendour along the line of my life.
But the congregation of clouds paces in dolour
Over my head and her never barren belly
Where we lie, summered, together, a world and I.
Her birdflecked hair, sunsetting the weather,
Feathers my eye, she shakes an ear-ring sky,

GEORGE And her hand of a country trembles against me.
BARKER The glittering nightriders gambol through
    A zodiac of symbols above our love
    Promising, O my star-crossed, death and disasters.
    But I want breath for nothing but your possession
    Now, now, this summer midnight, before the dawn
    Shakes its bright gun in the sky, before
    The serried battalions of lies and organizations of hate
    Entirely encompass us, buried; before the wolf and friend
    Render us enemies. Before all this,
    Lie one night in my arms and give me peace.

WILLIAM BELL

A YOUNG MAN'S SONG

(Pastourelle)

Maidens who this bursting May
Through the woods in quaint distress
Wander till you find your way,
Attend to what I have to say,
    But ask me nothing,
    Ask me nothing,
Ask me nothing you can guess.

Here I learned a year ago
This burden from a shepherdess:
'Love is wakefulness and woe;
'Where he hurts you ought to know,
    'So ask me nothing,
    'Ask me nothing,
'Ask me nothing you can guess'.

'My dear,' said I, 'when you complain
'You cry to courtesy for redress:
'May not I avenge your pain?'
But still she sang the same refrain,
    'Ask me nothing,
    'Ask me nothing,
'Ask me nothing you can guess'.

In that thicket where we hid
We found a primrose-bank to press,
And there I served her as she bid.

Let me shew you what we did!
>But ask me nothing,
>Ask me nothing,
Ask me nothing you can guess.

ELEGY VIII

Silent is Orpheus now, and silent now
the lyre you strung within a turtle shell,
which made the cypresses and mountains bow
and moved the violent guardians of Hell.
Here where the sea makes thunder in this cave,
>your musical ear, whose glooms
>contemptuously refuse
the day's enquiry, the descending Muse
>in vain spreads her miraculous plumes
forming like foam upon a breaking wave.

You are the climber who became aware
suddenly, of the mute hostility
of mountains; as the wind plucked at your hair,
balanced between the known and the unknown
>you turned, and knew yourself to be
frozen and weary and alone, alone.

Now that the mountains and the quiet lake
threaten no longer, you have found no peace,
only this most uneasy armistice,
even at night, when you will lie awake
watching the darkness, listening to the silence,
or fight to keep your balance
upon the polished buttress of your dream.
>You hug the stone
but that most cold composure is unbroken
>even at night, when you awaken
sober and thirsty and alone, alone.

WILLIAM
BELL

    That silence will not stop,
  although you stop your ear with clay,
although you put your mouth to every cup,
even the hemlock of the philosopher,
    and drink it up,
her name will be the last you breathe away.
    There is no end of her
    who haunts your mouth and ears.
Only the soft pulsation of a note
of music comforts them, as if you float
  upon the ocean's heaving breast
    or share in the remote
reiterated motion of the spheres.
For Aphrodite fills those instruments
whose very imperfections she acclaims;
the viola and the violin, caressed
like children, and the violoncello, pressed
most like a lover to her eager limbs.
She brings no sudden trumpet for alarms
  but comes with flutes and lyres,
    desiring thus to summon
the various treacheries of your desires
    to arms, to arms,
against the ideal image of a woman.
    How many trembling heroes come
in secret, joining that rebellion!
    Indeed, I cannot tell
      how many million
gain the reward of martyrdom
or cling together in the cold of Hell.

O when you played your music seemed unending,
  and then at your commands
    legions of angels descending
would succour you, or bear you in their hands.

WILLIAM BELL

But now the rejoicing choirs stand apart
watching the judgment that you do not fear:
thunder across the ranges of your heart,
salt water filling the musical mouth and ear.
    Now you are lost
to the confederation of the weathers
    which lay your body bare
    and cover you with frost,
even with those miraculous feathers
forming like frost in the unruffled air.

ELEGY XII

Tonight the moon is high, to summon all
the scholars, they who herald and who praise
all things beneath the ruling moon—the shaming
distempers of our blood; the rise and fall
of history with every added tear:-
to summon all the trumpeters, proclaiming
    love from a higher sphere,
  whom they pursue beyond our gaze;
out of their dream of drowning to call them here
to find the moonlit city they must raise.

Along the level sands, bathed by her beams,
the passionate men who wander by the sea
pour to the waves the torrent of their troubles,
their tears more cold than the Norwegian streams.
Lear with marigolds in his silver hair
follows the curve of the abandoned bubbles,
    Tristram in his despair
  watches the empty line of sky,
and Timon as he sniffs the salty air
curses the stink of all humanity.

WILLIAM BELL

Tonight I watched those lonely heroes weep
the interruption of their own delight,
and comforted myself: you are no woman
if you would mourn a friend who fell asleep,
charmed by the ocean's music, till the theme
grew tyrannous, the trumpeter inhuman.
    I think he had his dream
  without regretting, but tonight
all men are carried on a freezing stream
or wander weeping in the cold moonlight.

That moon could tell, we all must lie alone
at last among the tides of time and space.
Why do we mourn the dead? we do not pity
the million ammonites transformed to stone
and tossed about by the same pitiless hand
that casts the carven fragments of a city
    like shells upon the sand.
  Yet history's austere embrace
has only covered him that he may sand
far purer than the moon's inconstant face,

that he may stand before our Parthenon
with every flaw we fancied washed away,
so that the surging crowds of the forgiven
may flow about his plinth, or climb upon
the platform, gazing where his face appears
as if the crescent moon were fixed in heaven.
    The tribute of your tears
  and tongues is all that you can pay;
water and songs tumble toward his ears
to cover us tomorrow or today,

for this is the fulfilment of your dreams,
desire that was as stealthy as a dew
now openly from the obedient ocean

WILLIAM invokes his tide, and from the hills their streams.
   BELL In the overflowing bay, among
        the drifting ships, leaping in their devotion,
      a thousand dolphins throng,
     and with the same devotion you
no longer flee the destroying flood of song,
the music of the scholars, but pursue,

pursue the flowing trumpet till you see,
more generous than the tritons of a spring,
the steadfast heralds, drowned in blood and bleeding,
who still proclaim: 'the tide of history
must drown the glittering city of the mind,
but in remotest centuries receding
      will leave a coast behind,
    where once again the brooks will sing,
where in his nets the fisherman will find
a triton's marble mouth still trumpeting.'

But do not watch the moon's enraging face.
For all our folly nothing intercedes
save only Love. Love is another planet
islanded in the purity of space,
but there upon that island, torn or hewed
or grown miraculously from the granite,
      eternally pursued,
   upon his saltire Andrew bleeds,
preaching to the obedient multitude,
and the moon dips and drowns, but no man heeds.

JOHN BETJEMAN

PARLIAMENT HILL FIELDS

Rumbling under blackened girders, Midland, bound
 for Cricklewood,
Puffed its sulphur to the sunset where that Land of
 Laundries stood.
Rumble under, thunder over, train and tram alternate
 go,
Shake the floor and smudge the ledger, Charrington,
 Sells, Dale and Co.,
Nuts and nuggets in the window, trucks along the
 lines below.

When the Bon Marché was shuttered, when the feet
 were hot and tired,
Outside Charrington's we waited, by the 'STOP
 HERE IF REQUIRED',
Launched aboard the shopping basket, sat
 precipitately down,
Rocked past Zwanziger the Baker's, and the terrace
 blackish brown,
And the Anglo, Anglo-Norman Parish Church of
 Kentish Town.

Till the tram went over thirty, sighting terminus
 again,
Past municipal lawn tennis and the bobble-
 hanging plane;
Soft the light suburban evening caught our ashlar-
 speckled spire,
Eighteen-sixty Early English, as the mighty elms
 retire,

JOHN BETJE-MAN

Either side of Brookfield Mansions flashing fine
French-window fire.
Oh, the after tram ride quiet, when we heard a mile
beyond,
Silver music from the bandstand, barking dogs by
Highgate Pond;
Up the hill where stucco houses in Virginia creeper
drown;
And my childish wave of pity, seeing children
carrying down
Sheaves of drooping dandelions to the courts of
Kentish Town.

UPPER LAMBOURNE

Up the ash tree climbs the ivy,
   Up the ivy climbs the sun.
With a twenty thousand pattering
   Has a valley breeze begun,
Feathery ash, neglected elder,
   Shift the shade and make it run—

Shift the shade towards the nettles,
   And the nettles set it free
To streak the stained Cararra headstone
   Where, in nineteen-twenty-three,
He who trained a hundred winners
   Paid the Final Entrance Fee.

Leathery limbs of Upper Lambourne,
   Leathery skin from sun and wind,
Leathery breeches, spreading stables,
   Shining saddles left behind,
To the down the string of horses
   Moving out of sight and mind.

Feathery ash in leathery Lambourne
   Waves above the sarsen stone,
And Edwardian plantations
   So coniferously moan
As to make the swelling downland,
   Far surrounding, seem their own.

JOHN BETJEMAN

YOUTH AND AGE ON BEAULIEU RIVER, HANTS.

Early sun on Beaulieu water
   Lights the undersides of oaks,
Clumps of leaves it floods and blanches
All transparent glow the branches
   Which the double sunlight soaks;
And to her craft on Beaulieu water
Clemency the General's daughter
   Pulls across with even strokes.

Schoolboy sure she is this morning;
   Soon her sharpie's rigg'd and free.
Cool beneath a garden awning
   Mrs Fairclough sipping tea
And raising large long-distance glasses
As the little sharpie passes,
   Sighs our sailor girl to see:

Tulip figure, so appealing,
   Oval face, so serious-eyed,
Tree-roots pass'd and muddy beaches,
On to huge and lake-like reaches,
   Soft and sun-warm, see her glide,
Slacks the slim young limbs revealing,
Sun-brown arm the tiller feeling,
   Before the wind and with the tide.

JOHN
BETJE-
MAN

Evening light will bring the water,
   Day-long sun will burst the bud,
Clemency, the General's daughter,
   Will return upon the flood.
But the older woman only
Knows the ebb tide leaves her lonely
   With the shining fields of mud.

LAURENCE BINYON

VIRGIL'S FAREWELL TO DANTE
(Purgatorio, Canto XXVII)

Already, through the splendour ere the morn,
   Which to wayfarers the more grateful shows,
   Lodging less far from home, where they return,
The shadows on all sides were fleeing, and close
   On them my sleep fled; wherefore, having seen
   The great masters risen already, I rose.
'That apple whose sweetness in their craving keen
   Mortals go seeking on so many boughs
   This day shall peace to all thy hungers mean.'
Words such as these to me did Virgil use;
   And no propitious gifts did man acquire
   For pleasure matching these, to have or choose.
So came on me desire upon desire
   To be above, that now with every tread
   I felt wings on me growing to waft me higher.
When under us the whole high stair was sped
   And we unto the topmost step had won,
   Virgil, fixing his eyes upon me, said:
'The temporal and the eternal fire, my son,
   Thou hast beheld: thou art come now to a part
   Where of myself I see no farther on.
I have brought thee hither both by wit and art.
   Take for thy guide thine own heart's pleasure now.
   Forth from the narrows, from the steeps, thou art.
See there the sun that shines upon thy brow;
   See the young grass, the flowers and coppices
   Which this soil, of itself alone, makes grow.
While the fair eyes are coming, full of bliss,

Which weeping made me come to thee before,
Amongst them thou canst go or sit at ease.
Expect from me no word or signal more.
Thy will is upright, sound of tissue, free:
To disobey it were a fault; wherefore
Over thyself I crown thee and mitre thee.'

THOMAS BLACKBURN

OEDIPUS

His shadow monstrous on the palace wall,
That swollen boy, fresh from his mother's arms,
The odour of her body on his palms,
Moves to the eyeless horror of the hall.

And with what certainty the Revelation
Gropes for the sage's lips; a whining bark
Breaks from that crumpled linen in the dark,
To name the extremity of violation.

How should he not but tremble as the world
Contracts about him to his mother's room,
Red-curtained, stifling; in the firelit gloom
His bloated manhood on her bed is curled.

Then up and blind him, hands, pull blackness down
And let this woman on the strangling cord
Hang in the rich embroidery of her gown;
Then up and blind him, pull the blackness down.

But as he stumbles to the desert sands,
Bleeding and helpless as the newly born,
His daughters leading him with childish hands,
I see beyond all words his future shape,
Its feet upon the carcass of the ape
And round its mighty head, prophetic birds.

THE MIDNIGHT SKATERS

The hop-poles stand in cones,
The icy pond lurks under,
The pole-tops steeple to the thrones
Of stars, sound gulfs of wonder;
But not the tallest there, 'tis said,
Could fathom to this pond's black bed.

Then is not death at watch
Within those secret waters?
What wants he but to catch
Earth's heedless sons and daughters?
With but a crystal parapet
Between, he has his engines set.

Then on, blood shouts, on, on,
Twirl, wheel whip above him,
Dance on this ball-floor thin and wan,
Use him as though you love him;
Court him, elude him, reel and pass,
And let him hate you through the glass.

REPORT ON EXPERIENCE

I have been young, and now am not too old;
And I have seen the righteous forsaken,
His health, his honour and his quality taken.
This is not what we were formerly told.

I have seen a green country, useful to the race,   EDMUND
Knocked silly with guns and mines, its villages   BLUNDEN
    vanished,
Even the last rat and the last kestrel banished—
   God bless us all, this was peculiar grace.

I knew Seraphina; Nature gave her hue,
Glance, sympathy, note, like one from Eden.
I saw her smile warp, heard her lyric deaden;
   She turned to harlotry;—this I took to be new.

Say what you will, our God sees how they run.
These disillusions are His curious proving
That He loves humanity and will go on loving;
   Over there are faith, life, virtue in the sun.

SOLUTIONS

The swallow flew like lightning over the green
And through the gate-bars (a hand's breadth
    between);
He hurled his blackness at that chink and won;
The problem scarcely rose and it was done.

The spider, chance-confronted with starvation,
Took up another airy situation;
His working legs, as it appeared to me,
Had mastered practical geometry.

The old dog dreaming in his frowsy cask
Enjoyed his rest and did not drop his task;
He knew the person of 'no fixed abode',
And challenged as he shuffled down the road.

EDMUND These creatures which (Buffon and I agree)
BLUNDEN Lag far behind the human faculty
        Worked out the question set with satisfaction
        And promptly took the necessary action.

By this successful sang-froid I, employed
On 'Who wrote Shakespeare?' justly felt annoyed,
And seeing an evening primrose by the fence
Beheaded it for blooming insolence.

THE GIANT PUFFBALL

From what proud star I know not, but I found
Myself newborn below the coppice rail,
No bigger than the dewdrops and as round,
In a soft sward, no cattle might assail.

And here I gathered mightiness and grew
With this one dream kindling in me: that I
Should never cease from conquering light and dew
Till my white splendour touched the trembling sky.

A century of blue and stilly light
Bowed down before me, the dew came agen,
The moon my sibyl worshipped through the night,
The sun returned and long revered: but then

Hoarse drooping darkness hung me with a shroud
And switched at me with shrivelled leaves in scorn:
Red morning stole beneath a grinning cloud,
And suddenly clambering over dike and thorn

EDMUND BLUNDEN

A half-moon host of churls with flags and sticks
Hallooed and hurtled up the partridge brood,
And Death clapped hands from all the echoing thicks,
And trampling envy spied me where I stood;

Who haled me tired and quaking, hid me by,
And came agen after an age of cold,
And hung me in the prison-house a-dry
From the great crossbeam. Here defiled and old

I perish through unnumbered hours, I swoon,
Hacked with harsh knives to staunch a child's torn
    hand;
And all my hopes must with my body soon
Be but as crouching dust and wind-blown sand.

WILFRID SCAWEN BLUNT

A STORM IN SUMMER

Nature that day a woman was in weakness,
A woman in her impotent high wrath.
At the dawn we watched it, a low cloud half seen
Under the sun; an innocent child's face
It seemed to us rose-red and fringed with light
Boding no hurt, a pure translucent cloud,
Deep in the East where the Sun's disk began.
We did not guess what strengths in it were pent,
What terrors of rebellion. An hour more,
And it had gathered volume and the form
Of a dark mask, the she-wolf's of old Rome,
The ears, the brow, the cold unpitying eyes,
Through which gleams flashed. And, as we watched, the roll
Of thunder from a red throat muttering
Gave menace of the wild beast close at hand.
Anon a wall of darkness in the South
Black to the zenith, and a far-off wail,
The wind among the trees.—And then, behold,
Flying before it a mad clamorous rout
Of peewits, starlings, hawks, crows, dishwashers,
Blackbirds and jays, by hundreds, scattering,
While the Earth trembled holding as it were its breath;
Till suddenly an answer from the ground,
And the fields shook and a new mighty roar
Crashed through the oaks, and in a pent-up flow
The storm's rage broke in thunder overhead,
And all the anger of the passionate heaven
Burst into tears.

ROBERT BRIDGES

THE PSALM

While Northward the hot sun was sinking o'er the trees
as we sat pleasantly talking in the meadow,
the swell of a rich music suddenly on our ears
gush'd thru' the wide-flung doors, where village-folk in church
stood to their evening psalm praising God together—
and when it came to cloze, paused, and broke forth anew.

A great Huguenot psalm it trod forth on the air
with full slow notes moving as a goddess stepping
through the responsive figures of a stately dance
conscious of beauty and of her fair-flowing array
in the severe perfection of an habitual grace,
then stooping to its cloze, paused to dance forth anew;

To unfold its bud of melody everlastingly
fresh as in springtime when, four centuries agone,
it wing'd the souls of martyrs on their way to heav'n
chain'd at the barbarous stake, mid the burning faggots
standing with tongues cut out, all singing in the flames—
O evermore, sweet Psalm, shalt thou break forth anew.

Thou, when in France that self-idolatrous idol reign'd
that starv'd his folk to fatten his priests and concubines,

ROBERT BRIDGES thou wast the unconquerable paean of resolute men
who fell in coward massacre or with Freedom fled
from the palatial horror into far lands away,
and England learnt to voice thy deathless strain anew.

Ah! they endured beyond worst pangs of fire and steel
torturings invisible of tenderness and untold;
No Muse may name them, nay, no man will whisper them;
sitting alone he dare not think of them—and wail
of babes and mothers' wail flouted in ribald song.
Draw to thy cloze, sweet Psalm, pause and break forth anew!

Thy minstrels were no more, yet thy triumphing plaint
haunted their homes, as once in a deserted house
in Orthes, as 'twas told, the madden'd soldiery
burst in and search'd but found nor living man nor maid
only the sound flow'd round them and desisted not
but when it wound to cloze, paused, and broke forth anew.

And oft again in some lone valley of the Cevennes
where unabsolvèd crime yet calleth plagues on France
thy heavenly voice would lure the bloodhounds on, astray,
hunting their fancied prey afar in the dark night
and with its ghostly music mock'd their oaths and knives.
O evermore great Psalm spring forth! spring forth anew!

GHOSTS

ROBERT BRIDGES

Mazing around my mind like moths at a shaded
   candle.
   In my heart like lost bats in a cave fluttering,
Mock ye the charm whereby I thought reverently to
   lay you,
   When to the wall I nail'd your reticent effigys?

'Ετώσιον ἄχθος ἀρούρης

Who goes there? God knows. I'm nobody. How
   should I answer?
   Can't jump over a gate nor run across the meadow.
I'm but an old whitebeard of inane identity. Pass on!
   What's left of me to-day will very soon be nothing.

THE FUNERAL OF YOUTH: THRENODY

The day that *Youth* had died,
There came to his grave-side,
In decent mourning, from the county's ends,
Those scatter'd friends
Who had liv'd the boon companions of his prime,
And laugh'd with him and sung with him and wasted,
In feast and wine and many-crown'd carouse,
The days and nights and dawnings of the time
When *Youth* kept open house,
Nor left untasted
Aught of his high emprise and ventures dear,
No quest of his unshar'd—
All these, with loitering feet and sad head bar'd,
Follow'd their old friend's bier.
Folly went first,
With muffled bells and coxcomb still revers'd;
And after trod the bearers, hat in hand—
Laughter, most hoarse, and Captain *Pride* with tann'd
And martial face all grim, and fussy *Joy*,
Who had to catch a train, and *Lust*, poor, snivelling boy;
These bore the dear departed.
Behind them, broken-hearted,
Came *Grief*, so noisy a widow, that all said,
'Had he but wed
Her elder sister *Sorrow*, in her stead!'
And by her, trying to soothe her all the time,
The fatherless children, *Colour*, *Tune*, and *Rhyme*
(The sweet lad *Rhyme*), ran all-uncomprehending.

Then, at the way's sad ending,
Round the raw grave they stay'd. Old *Wisdom* read,
In mumbling tone, the Service for the Dead.
There stood *Romance*,
The furrowing tears had mark'd her rougèd cheek;
Poor old *Conceit*, his wonder unassuag'd;
Dead *Innocency's* daughter, *Ignorance*;
And shabby, ill-dress'd *Generosity*;
And *Argument*, too full of woe to speak;
Passion, grown portly, something middle-aged;
And *Friendship*—not a minute older, she;
Impatience, ever taking out his watch;
Faith, who was deaf, and had to lean, to catch
Old *Wisdom's* endless drone.
Beauty was there,
Pale in her black; dry-ey'd; she stood alone.
Poor maz'd *Imagination*; *Fancy* wild;
Ardour, the sunlight on his greying hair;
Contentment, who had known *Youth* as a child
And never seen him since. And *Spring* came too,
Dancing over the tombs, and brought him flowers—
She did not stay for long.
And *Truth*, and *Grace*, and all the merry crew,
The laughing *Winds* and *Rivers*, and lithe *Hours*;
And *Hope*, the dewy-ey'd; and sorrowing *Song*;—
Yes, with much woe and mourning general,
At dead *Youth's* funeral,
Even these were met once more together, all,
Who erst the fair and living *Youth* did know;
All, except only *Love*. *Love* had died long ago.

RUPERT
BROOKE

EL AGHIR

Sprawled on the bags and crates in the rear of the truck,
I was gummy-mouthed from the sun and the dust of the track;
And the two Arab soldiers I'd taken on as hitch-hikers,
At a torrid petrol-dump, had been there on their hunkers
Since early morning. I said, in a kind of French,
'On m'a dit qu'il y a une belle source d'eau fraîche,
Plus loin, à El Aghir.'
                        It was eighty more kilometres
Until round a corner we heard a splashing of waters,
And there, in a green, dark street, was a fountain with two facets,
Discharging both ways, from full-throated faucets,
Into basins, thence into troughs and thence into brooks.
Our negro corporal driver slammed his brakes,
And we yelped and leapt from the truck and went at the double
To fill our bidons and bottles and drink and dabble.
Then, swollen with water, we went to an inn for wine.
The Arabs came too, though their creed might have stood between:
'After all,' they said, 'it's a boisson,' without contrition.

Green, green is El Aghir. It has a railway station,
And the wealth of its soil has borne many another fruit:

A mairie, a school and an elegant Salle de Fêtes.
Such blessings, as I remarked, in effect, to the waiter,
Are added unto them that have plenty of water.

NORMAN CAMERON

THE FIRM OF HAPPINESS, LIMITED

The Firm of Happiness, Limited, was one to astonish the stars,
More like a thriving town than a multiple store—a hotchpotch
Of markets and playrooms and chapels and brothels and baths and bars,
As smoothly running and closely packed as the works of a watch.

Nobody finally understood the cause of the crash.
Some spoke of Nemesis; others rumoured, vaguely, of course,
That a gang of Directors had simply robbed the firm of its cash,
Or that some ironical Jew was selling it short on the Bourse.

Whatever the reason, the firm of a sudden began to fail.
The floors were undusted at corners, the commissionaires were unshaved,
The girls were anxious and raucous, the comedians' jokes were stale.
The customers noticed the difference—to judge from the way they behaved.

NORMAN CAMERON When Happiness closed its doors, the Corporation of the city
    Were distressed to see so vast a property left alone
    To moulder and waste; in a mingled impulse of thrift and pity
    They decided to buy the empty building, and floated a loan.

Now nobody knows what to do with this monstrous hulk we have bought.
At the last Corporation meeting one alderman, half in jest,
Spoke of turning it into a barracks. Meanwhile there's the dreary thought
That we ratepayers have to keep paying the burdensome interest.

THREE LOVE POEMS

I

From a Woman to a Greedy Lover

What is this recompense you'd have from me?
Melville asked no compassion of the sea.
Roll to and fro, forgotten in my rack,
Love as you please—I owe you nothing back.

II

In the Queen's Room

In the smoky outhouses of the court of love
I chattered, a recalcitrant underling
Living on scraps. 'Below stairs or above,
All's one,' I said. 'We valets have our fling.'

Now I am come, by a chance beyond reach,
Into your room, my body smoky and soiled
And on my tongue the taint of chattering speech,
Tell me, Queen, am I irredeemably spoiled?

III
Shepherdess

All day my sheep have mingled with yours. They strayed
Into your valley seeking a change of ground.
Held and bemused with what they and I had found,
Pastures and wonders, heedlessly I delayed.

Now it is late. The tracks leading home are steep,
The stars and landmarks in your country are strange.
How can I take my sheep back over the range?
Shepherdess, show me now where I may sleep.

ROY CAMPBELL

TOLEDO, JULY 1936

Toledo, when I saw you die
And heard the roof of Carmel crash,
A spread-winged phoenix from its ash
The Cross remained against the sky!
With horns of flame and haggard eye
The mountain vomited with blood,
A thousand corpses down the flood
Were rolled gesticulating by,
And high above the roaring shells
I heard the silence of your bells
Who've left these broken stones behind
Above the years to make your home,
And burn, with Athens and with Rome,
A sacred city of the mind.

THE SISTERS

After hot loveless nights, when cold winds stream
Sprinkling the frost and dew, before the light,
Bored with the foolish things that girls must dream
Because their beds are empty of delight,

Two sisters rise and strip. Out from the night
Their horses run to their low-whistled pleas—
Vast phantom shapes with eyeballs rolling white
That sneeze a fiery steam about their knees:

Through the crisp manes their stealthy prowling hands,
Stronger than curbs, in slow caresses rove,

They gallop down across the milk-white sands
And wade far out into the sleeping cove:

The frost stings sweetly with a burning kiss
As intimate as love, as cold as death:
Their lips, whereon delicious tremors hiss,
Fume with the ghostly pollen of their breath.

Far out on the grey silence of the flood
They watch the dawn in smouldering gyres expand
Beyond them: and the day burns through their blood
Like a white candle through a shuttered hand.

CHOOSING A MAST

This mast, new-shaved, through whom I rive the ropes,
Says she was once an oread of the slopes,
Graceful and tall upon the rocky highlands,
A slender tree as vertical as noon,
And her low voice was lovely as the silence
Through which a fountain whistles to the moon,
Who now of the white spray must take the veil
And, for her songs, the thunder of the sail.

I chose her for her fragrance, when the spring
With sweetest resins swelled her fourteenth ring
And with live amber welded her young thews:
I chose her for the glory of the Muse,
Smoother of forms, that her hard-knotted grain,
Grazed by the chisel, shaven by the plane,
Might from the steel as cool a burnish take
As from the bladed moon a windless lake.

Roy Camp-bell
I chose her for her eagerness of flight
Where she stood tiptoe on the rocky height
Lifted by her own perfume to the sun,
  While through her rustling plumes with eager sound
  Her eagle spirit, with the gale at one,
  Spreading wide pinions, would have spurned the ground
  And her own sleeping shadow, had they not
  With thymy fragrance charmed her to the spot.

Lover of song, I chose this mountain pine
Not only for the straightness of her spine
But for her songs: for there she loved to sing
Through a long noon's repose of wave and wing,
The fluvial swirling of her scented hair
Sole rill of song in all that windless air,
And her slim form the naiad of the stream
Afloat upon the languor of its theme;

And for the soldier's fare on which she fed:
Her wine the azure, and the snow her bread;
And for her stormy watches on the height,
For only out of solitude or strife
Are born the sons of valour and delight;
And lastly for her rich exulting life,
That with the wind stopped not its singing breath
But carolled on, the louder for its death.

Under a pine, when summer days were deep,
We loved the most to lie in love or sleep:
And when in long hexameters the west
Rolled his grey surge, the forest for his lyre,
It was the pines that sang us to our rest,
Loud in the wind and fragrant in the fire,

With legioned voices swelling all night long,
From Pelion to Provence, their storm of song.

It was the pines that fanned us in the heat,
The pines, that cheered us in the time of sleet,
For which sweet gifts I set one dryad free;
No longer to the wind a rooted foe,
This nymph shall wander where she longs to be
And with the blue north wind arise and go,
A silver huntress with the moon to run
And fly through rainbows with the rising sun;

And when to pasture in the glittering shoals
The guardian mistral drives his thundering foals,
And when like Tartar horsemen racing free
We ride the snorting fillies of the sea,
My pine shall be the archer of the gale
While on the bending willow curves the sail
From whose great bow the long keel shooting home
Shall fly, the feathered arrow of the foam.

LUIS DE CAMÕES

Camões, alone, of all the lyric race,
Born in the black aurora of disaster,
Can look a common soldier in the face:
I find a comrade where I sought a master:
For daily, while the stinking crocodiles
Glide from the mangroves on the swampy shore,
He shares my awning on the dhow, he smiles,
And tells me that he lived it all before.
Through fire and shipwreck, pestilence and loss,
Led by the ignis fatuus of duty

ROY CAMPBELL To a dog's death—yet of his sorrows king—
He shouldered high his voluntary Cross,
Wrestled his hardships into forms of beauty,
And taught his gorgon destinies to sing.

MAURICE CARPENTER

TO S.T.C. ON HIS 179TH BIRTHDAY, OCTOBER 12TH, 1951

There's a brief spring in all of us and when it finishes
The winter must be faced; an uncreative
Dying into darkness, sudden and
Horrible in the line of the face,
Balding, a baggy abdomen, laughable, abominable!
Imagine the horror in the mirror! Can there be any
Resurrection after the final realisation
Of down-descent, the reversal of creation?

I have seen snow in April blow across
Hopes; blossoms made Neapolitan, pink cherry
Loaded with cold white crystals, pretty
Confectionery, delicate ambiguity,
As you in Germany suffered a treeless spring,
Snowbound nightingales and a dead child
Coffined in heart's abstraction. You returned
To a ten year chaos, uncreative burning

Of an unfuelled furnace. A belated Beatrice
Nursed the moment they deserted you.
Names. Codes. New handwritings. A new
Start. The letters jumbled up, disguised as Greek,
Fallen abroad, all abroad. The Friend has folded
Its final pages. The crumpled ages speak
Bitterly. I feel about my neck
The Albatross of your inexpiable guilt.

Can there be resurrection after ten years'
Disintegration, newspapers, public life

MAURICE CARPENTER

On a brassy island, walls and no shadows?
The duty and the dispathetic wife
Nag in the mind. Insure your fears
As children die in fantasy. Widowhood
Wanted, the widower wandering.
Talk to locked notebooks wet with tears.

No catalyst, no critical temperature
For the chemical change that flashes in a poem;
A universe of machine components; no
Embodied or embodying whole, living and growing.
The moon that smiled from a sky of opium
No more benign, changed to an inward horror.
Precision of an engine out of action. Given
Such a broken loom, can a new cloth be woven?

Forsaken a moment by the same shaping
Spirit behind the ship, the soul, cold wax,
Congeals on a brass horizon: Imagination
Is walking a narrow gangplank, swaying
Above the milk of the abyss; stations
Of stars, the harbour is at our backs.
The South Pole of our Peace recedes, recedes;
The North Pole of our fear comes nearer, nearer.

Extremes meet. Love is a sudden image,
Agate, unchanging, neither wife nor mother;
A sharp chord in the silence, woman bending over
Children; voices grope for mysteries
Of first speech, minting words and worlds.
The world we know and the world we dream forever
Disparate, a double candle flame.
Can they coincide and be the same?

MAURICE CARPENTER

What more than you can we do? Such love is vulnerable
To the knock of neutrons and the nerve of want.
Friend, on your hundred and seventy ninth
Birthday I turn to you. Could you foresee
The world discarded like a ball of paper?
The hate we face more dangerous, our roots no deeper.
The Lady in the silence bares her dugs
And draws us down to her warm and genial mud.

Needled by no insomnia my sleep is deep.
The nightmare lies in the century's rough kip,
And all the stars upon my childhood ceiling
Fade, flake off; the cradle of the earth
Sways in a void between receding stars.
Neighbour to Venus by a wrinkled Mars,
Our spring delayed, and each demanding birth
Weighs down the walls of our insubstantial dwelling.

Esteecee I have left you while I listed
Our own worries: they were yours as well.
World, word within, the man as child
Delights in future even as eye grows dull.
The bird falls. The weight is at our neck.
The body swings by the idly flapping wheel.
In the roads outside a Jonah century
You paused, and smelled the darkness we know well.

A BALLAD FOR KATHARINE
OF ARAGON

As I walked down by the river
Down by the frozen fen
I saw the grey cathedral
With the eyes of a child of ten.
O the railway arch is smoky
As the Flying Scot goes by
And but for the Education Act
Go Jumper Cross and I.

But war is a bitter bugle
That all must learn to blow
And it didn't take long to stop the song
In the dirty Italian snow.
O war is a casual mistress
And the world is her double bed
She has a few charms in her mechanised arms
But you wake up and find yourself dead.

The olive tree in winter
Casts her banner down
And the priest in white and scarlet
Comes up from the muddy town.
O never more will Jumper
Watch the Flying Scot go by
His funeral knell was a six-inch shell
Singing across the sky.

The Queen of Castile has a daughter
Who won't come home again

CHARLES
CAUSLEY

She lies in the grey cathedral
Under the arms of Spain.
O the Queen of Castile has a daughter
Torn out by the roots
Her lovely breast in a cold stone chest
Under the farmers' boots.

Now I like a Spanish party
And many O many the day
I have watched them swim as the night came dim
In Algeciras Bay.
O the high sierra was thunder
And the seven-branched river of Spain
Came down to the sea to plunder
The heart of the sailor again.

O shall I leap in the river
And knock upon paradise door
For a gunner of twenty-seven and a half
And a queen of twenty-four?
From the almond tree by the river
I watch the sky with a groan
For Jumper and Kate are always out late
And I lie here alone.

G. K. CHESTERTON

THE OLD SONG

(On the Embankment in Stormy Weather)

A livid sky on London
And like the iron steeds that rear
A shock of engines halted,
And I knew the end was near:
And something said that far away, over the hills and
    far away,
There came a crawling thunder and the end of all
    things here.
For London Bridge is broken down, broken down,
    broken down,
As digging lets the daylight on the sunken streets of
    yore,
The lightning looked on London town, the broken
    bridge of London town,
The ending of a broken road where men shall go no
    more.

I saw the kings of London town,
The kings that buy and sell,
That built it up with penny loaves,
And penny lies as well:
And where the streets were paved with gold the
    shrivelled paper shone for gold,
The scorching light of promises that pave the streets
    of hell.
For penny loaves will melt away, melt away, melt
    away,

Mock the mean that haggled in the grain they did not grow;
With hungry faces in the gate, a hundred thousand in the gate,
A thunder-flash on London and the finding of the foe.

G. K. CHESTERTON

I heard the hundred pin-makers
Slow down their racking din,
Till in the stillness men could hear
The dropping of a pin:
And somewhere men without the wall, beneath the wood, without the wall,
Had found the place where London ends and England can begin.
For pins and needles bend and break, bend and break, bend and break,
Faster than the breaking spears or the bending of the bow,
Of pageants pale in thunder-light, 'twixt thunder-load and thunder-light,
The Hundreds marching on the hills in the wars of long ago.

I saw great Cobbett riding,
The horseman of the shires;
And his face was red with judgement
And a light of Luddite fires:
And south to Sussex and the sea the lights leapt up for liberty,
The trumpet of the yeomanry, the hammer of the squires;
For bars of iron rust away, rust away, rust away,
Rend before the hammer and the horseman riding in,

Crying that all men at the last, and at the worst and at the last,
Have found the place where England ends and England can begin.

His horse-hoofs go before you,
Far beyond your bursting tyres;
And time is bridged behind him
And our sons are with our sires.
A trailing meteor on the Downs he rides above the rotten towns,
The Horseman of Apocalypse, the Rider of the Shires.
For London Bridge is broken down, broken down, broken down;
Blown the horn of Huntingdon from Scotland to the sea—
... Only a flash of thunder-light, a flying dream of thunder-light,
Had shown under the shattered sky a people that were free.

THE SKELETON

Chattering finch and water-fly
Are not merrier than I;
Here among the flowers I lie
Laughing everlastingly.
No; I may not tell the best;
Surely, friends, I might have guessed
Death was but the good King's jest,
It was hid so carefully.

JACK CLEMO

THE BURNT BUSH

A bush was on that dump:
A single stain of green and gold
'Mid glacial whiteness fold on fold—
A fang of Nature from the cold
And clay-purged sand: denied a clump,
    She put forth one gorse-stump.

I climbed there with a girl:
We squatted in the cleft to watch
The clay-land shadows till a snatch
Of fun led her to strike a match
And set it to the twigs. A curl
    Of crackling flame, a swirl

Of smoke, and we were penned
Behind a knot of fire which licked
Along the bristly stems and flicked
Petals and thorns as ash that pricked
White gravel far below the bend
    We waited to descend.

The clay-face soon was bare.
A few charred twigs remained to show
That Nature's vein was dried: a slow
Thin pulse of smoke trailed in the glow
Of sunset as we climbed with care
    Down to the fresher air.

Jack Clemo

        Fresh too was my desire.
I looked upon her laughing play
There in the gully's winding way:
A dry cool breeze had bared her clay.
Rain fosters sap and fashions mire,
    But dry clay prompts the fire.

    She fired the gorse—fired too
One gnarled old bush of Adam's seed
Which in a cleft of naked need
Within my soul had fouled indeed
White purity, and as it grew
    Spread doubts in scent and hue.

    Her hand held mine—and then
The flame leapt in and burnt the bush:
My soul knew smoke and fire, then hush
Of clay delivered from the push
Of Nature's sap: now in God's ken
    I stand unsoiled again.

A. E. COPPARD

THE UNFORTUNATE MILLER

On windy days the mill
Turned with a will,
But on calm days it spread
Its four sails—dead.

The one-eyed miller man
Laments that ban,
And to the windless sky
Turning his vexed eye:

'God help,' he sadly says,
'This business;
A hundred days and more
The wind's forebore,

And lacking breezes I
Am bound to die;
The profit I've forgone
In offal and grist alone

Would have bought a cock and a hen,
A gilt for my pen,
And a row of asters planted
Just where I wanted;

But since the wind is still—
The devil take the mill!
Never it rains but pours—
Let's in-a-doors.'

A. E. COPPARD

So in-a-doors goes he
To see—alas, to see—
Not the scrapings of a pan or pot
In his famished cot.

The tap of the clock indoors,
The dusty floors,
His empty crock and purse,
Made bad seem worse.

He looked at himself in the glass—
How thin he was!
He looked at the time and date—
Too late! Too late!

And creeping again to the mill
That stood stone still,
He tied round his neck the loop
Of a long dark rope,

Drove a tenpenny nail
Into the mill's black sail,
Hung his watch on a shelf,
Then hung himself.

And lo, the wind came! Beshrew,
How the wind blew!
And the sails, with the miller dying,
Went flying, flying.

ANTHONY CRONIN

FOR A FATHER

With the exact length and pace of his father's stride
The son walks,
Echoes and intonations of his father's speech
Are heard when he talks.

Once when the table was tall,
And the chair a wood,
He absorbed his father's smile and carefully copied
The way that he stood.

He grew into exile slowly,
With pride and remorse,
In some ways better than his begetters,
In others worse.

And now having chosen, with strangers,
Half glad of his choice,
He smiles with his father's hesitant smile
And speaks with his voice.

JOHN DAVIDSON

THIRTY BOB A WEEK

I couldn't touch a stop and turn a screw,
And set the blooming world a-work for me,
Like such as cut their teeth—I hope, like you—
On the handle of a skeleton gold key;
I cut mine on a leek, which I eat every week:
I'm a clerk at thirty bob a week as you can see.

But I don't allow it's luck and all a toss;
There's no such thing as being starred and crossed;
It's just the power of some to be a boss,
And the bally power of others to be bossed:
I face the music sir; you bet I ain't a cur;
Strike me lucky if I don't believe I'm lost!

For like a mole I journey in the dark,
A-travelling along the underground
From my Pillar'd Halls and broad Suburban Park,
To come the daily dull official round;
And home again at night with my pipe all alight,
A-scheming how to count ten bob a pound.

And it's often very cold and very wet,
And my missus stitches towels for a hunks;
And the Pillar'd Halls is half of it to let—
Three rooms about the size of travelling trunks.
And we cough, my wife and I, to dislocate a sigh,
When the noisy little kids are in their bunks.

But you never hear her do a growl or whine,
For she's made of flint and roses, very odd;

And I've got to cut my meaning very fine,
Or I'd blubber, for I'm made of greens and sod:
So p'r'aps we are in Hell for all I can tell,
And lost and damn'd and serv'd up hot to God.

I ain't blaspheming, Mr. Silver-tongue;
I'm saying things a bit beyond your art:
Of all the rummy starts you ever sprung,
Thirty bob a week's the rummiest start!
With your science and your books and your theories
    about spooks,
Did you ever hear of looking in your heart?

I didn't mean your pocket, Mr., no:
I mean that having children and a wife,
With thirty bob on which to come and go,
Isn't dancing to the tabor and the fife:
When it doesn't make you drink, by Heaven! it makes
    you think,
And notice curious items about life.

I step into my heart and there I meet
A god-almighty devil singing small,
Who would like to shout and whistle in the street,
And squelch the passers flat against the wall;
If the whole world was a cake he had the power to
    take,
He would take it, ask for more, and eat it all.

And I meet a sort of simpleton beside,
The kind that life is always giving beans;
With thirty bob a week to keep a bride
He fell in love and married in his teens:
At thirty bob he stuck; but he knows it isn't luck:
He knows the seas are deeper than tureens.

JOHN
DAVID-
SON
  And the god-almighty devil and the fool
That meet me in the High Street on the strike,
When I walk about my heart a-gathering wool,
    Are my good and evil angels if you like.
    And both of them together in every kind of weather
    Ride me like a double-seated bike.

That's rough a bit and needs its meaning curled.
    But I have a high old hot 'un in my mind—
A most egregious notion of the world,
    That leaves your lightning 'rithmetic behind:
    I give it at a glance when I say 'There ain't no chance,
    Nor nothing of the lucky-lottery kind.'

And it's this way that I make it out to be:
    No fathers, mothers, countries, climates—none;
Not Adam was responsible for me,
    Nor society, nor systems, nary one:
    A little sleeping seed, I woke—I did, indeed—
    A million years before the blooming sun.

I woke because I thought the time had come;
    Beyond my will there was no other cause;
And everywhere I found myself at home,
    Because I chose to be the thing I was;
    And in whatever shape of mollusc or of ape
    I always went according to the laws.

I was the love that chose my mother out;
    I joined two lives and from the union burst;
My weakness and my strength without a doubt
    Are mine alone for ever from the first:
    It's just the very same with a difference in the name
    As 'Thy will be done.' You say it if you durst!

They say it daily up and down the land
As easy as you take a drink, it's true:
But the difficultest go to understand,
And the difficultest job a man can do,
Is to come it brave and meek with thirty bob a week,
And feel that that's the proper thing for you.

It's a naked child against a hungry wolf;
It's playing bowls upon a splitting wreck;
It's walking on a string across a gulf
With millstones fore-and-aft about your neck;
But the thing is daily done by many and many a one;
And we fall, face forward, fighting, on the deck.

JOHN DAVIDSON

DONALD DAVIE

ON BERTRAND RUSSELL'S 'PORTRAITS FROM MEMORY'

Those Cambridge generations, Russell's, Keynes' . . .
And mine? Oh mine was Wittgenstein's, no doubt:
Sweet pastoral, too, when some-one else explains,
Although my memories leave the eclogues out.

The clod's not bowed by sedentary years,
Yet, set by Thyrsis, he's a crippled man:
How singularly naked each appears,
Beside the other on this bosky plan.

Arrangements of the copse and cloister seem,
Although effective, still Utopian,
For groves find room, behind a leafy screen,
For sage and harvester, but not for man.

I wonder still which of the hemispheres
Infects the other, in this grassy globe;
The chumbling moth of Madingley, that blears
The labourer's lamp, destroys the scarlet robe.

It was the Muse that could not make her home
In that too thin and yet too sluggish air,
Too volatile to live among the loam,
Her sheaves too heavy for the talkers there.

W. H. DAVIES

THE TRUTH

Since I have seen a bird one day,
His head pecked more than half away;
That hopped about with but one eye,
Ready to fight again, and die—
Ofttimes since then their private lives
Have spoilt that joy their music gives.

So when I see this robin now,
Like a red apple on the bough,
And question why he sings so strong,
For love, or for the love of song;
Or sings, maybe, for that sweet rill
Whose silver tongue is never still—

Ah, now there comes this thought unkind,
Born of the knowledge in my mind:
He sings in triumph that last night
He killed his father in a fight;
And now he'll take his mother's blood—
The last strong rival for his food.

THE SEA

Her cheeks were white, her eyes were wild,
Her heart was with her sea-gone child.
'Men say you know and love the sea?
It is ten days, my child left me;
Ten days, and still he doth not come,
And I am weary of my home.'

**W. H.
DAVIES**

I thought of waves that ran the deep
And flashed like rabbits, when they leap,
The white part of their tails; the glee
Of captains that take brides to sea,
And own the ships they steer; how seas
Played leapfrog over ships with ease.

The great Sea-Wind, so rough and kind;
Ho, ho! his strength; the great Sea-Wind
Blows iron tons across the sea!
Ho, ho! his strength; how wild and free!
He breaks the waves, to our amaze,
Into ten thousand little sprays!

'Nay, have no fear'; I laughed with joy,
'That you have lost a sea-gone boy;
The Sea's wild horses, they are far
More safe than Land's tamed horses are;
They kick with padded hoofs, and bite
With teeth that leave no marks in sight.

'True, Waves will howl when, all day long,
The Wind keeps piping loud and strong;
For in ships' sails the wild Sea-Breeze
Pipes sweeter than your birds in trees;
But have no fear'—I laughed with joy,
'That you have lost a sea-gone boy.'

That night I saw ten thousand bones
Coffined in ships, in weeds and stones;
Saw how the Sea's strong jaws could take
Big iron ships like rats to shake;
Heard him still moan his discontent
For one man or a continent.

I saw that woman go from place
To place, hungry for her child's face;
I heard her crying, crying, crying;
Then, in a flash! saw the Sea trying,
With savage joy, and efforts wild,
To smash his rocks with a dead child.

W. H.
DAVIES

THE GALLIASS

'Tell me, tell me,
    Unknown stranger,
When shall I sight me
    That tall ship
On whose flower-wreathed counter is gilded,
    Sleep?'

'Landsman, landsman,
    Lynx nor kestrel
Ne'er shall descry from
    Ocean steep
That midnight-stealing, high-pooped galliass,
    Sleep.'

'Promise me, Stranger,
    Though I mark not
When cold night-tide's
    Shadows creep,
Thou wilt keep unwavering watch for *Sleep*'.

'Myriad the lights are,
    Wayworn landsman,
Rocking the dark through
    On the deep:
She alone burns none to prove her *Sleep*.'

NAPOLEON

WALTER DE LA MARE

'What is the world, O soldiers?
    It is I:
I, this incessant snow,
    This northern sky;
Soldiers, this solitude
    Through which we go
    Is I.'

THE FECKLESS DINNER PARTY

'Who are we waiting for?' '*Soup* burnt?' ... Eight—
  'Only the tiniest party.—Us!'
'Darling! Divine!' 'Ten minutes late—'
  'And my digest—''I'm *rav*enous!'

'"Toomes"?'—'Oh, he's new.' 'Looks crazed, I guess.'
  '"Married"—*Again*!' 'Well; more or less!'

'Dinner is *served*!' ' "Dinner is served"!'
  'Is served?' 'Is served.' 'Ah, yes.'

Dear Mr. Prout, will you take down
  The Lilith in leaf-green by the fire?
Blanche Ogleton? . . .' 'How coy a frown!—
  Hasn't she borrowed *Eve's* attire?'
Morose Old Adam!' 'Charmed—I vow.'
  'Come then, and meet her now.'

Now, Dr. Mallus—would you please?—
  Our daring poetess, Delia Seek?'
The lady with the bony knees?'
  'And—*entre nous*—less song than beak.'
Sharing her past with Simple Si—'
  '*Bare* facts! He'll blush!' 'Oh, fie!'

WALTER 'And *you*, Sir Nathan—false but fair!—
DE LA   That fountain of wit, Aurora Pert.'
MARE 'More wit than It, poor dear! But there...'
    'Pitiless Pacha! *And* such a flirt!'
    ' "Flirt"! Me?' 'Who else?' 'You here.... Who
        can...?'
    'In*corrig*ible man!'

'And now, Mr. Simon—little me!—
    Last and—' 'By no means least!' 'Oh, come!
What naughty, naughty flattery!
    Honey!—I *hear* the creature hum!'
'Sweets for the sweet, I always say!'
    ' "Always"?... We're last.' '*This* way?'...

'No sir; straight on, please.' 'I'd have vowed!—
    I came the other....' It's queer; I'm sure...'
'What frightful pictures!' 'Fiends!' 'The *crowd*!'
    'Such nudes!' 'I can't endure...'

'Yes, *there* they go.' 'Heavens! *Are* we right?'
    'Follow up closer!' ' "Prout"?—sand-blind!'
'This endless...' 'Who's turned down the light?'
    'Keep calm! They're close behind.'

'Oh, Dr. Mallus; what dismal stairs!'
    'I hate these old Victor...' 'Dry rot!'
'Darker and darker!' 'Fog!' 'The air's...'
    'Scarce breathable!' 'Hell! *What*?'

'The banister's gone!' 'It's deep; keep close!'
    'We're going down and down!' 'What fun!'
'Damp! Why my shoes...' 'It's slimy... Not *moss*!'
    'I'm freezing cold!' 'Let's run.'

'... Behind us. I'm giddy ...' 'The catacombs ...'
  'That shout!' 'Who's there?' 'I'm *alone*!' 'Stand
    back!'
'She said, Lead ...' 'Oh!' 'Where's Toomes?'
  '*Toomes*!' 'Toomes!'
'Stifling!' 'My skull will crack!'

'Sir Nathan! *Ai*!' '*I say*! *Toomes*! Prout!'
  'Where? Where?' ' "Our silks and fine array" ...'
'She's mad.' 'I'm dying!' 'Oh, let me *out*!'
  'My God! We've lost our way!' ...

And now how sad-serene the abandoned house,
Whereon at dawn the spring-tide sunbeams beat;
And time's slow pace alone is ominous,
And naught but shadows of noonday therein meet;
Domestic microcosm, only a Trump could rouse:
And, pondering darkly, in the silent rooms,
He who misled them all—the butler, Toomes.

C. M. DOUGHTY

HYMN TO THE SUN

(*From* The Dawn in Britain)

Sith, in dark speech, Carvilios hymn unfolds,
Of the day-god, known only to few druids:
How, sprung of womb of the Eternal Night;
Whence, daily, he, highest new-born god, upmounts,
Shaking his amber locks, and breathes sweet breath,
O'er plains of the low world. The virgin hours,
Before him, tracing, on their silver feet,
Open wide gates of heaven, where he doth pass.
In their cloud chariots, wont, against him, ride,
Then envious spirits of the misty murk.
But when, from his hot looks, those flee dispersed,
Rejoice again, all dwellers in the earth.
On heaven's steep hill, ascends the glorious path,
Of Belin's steeds. High-riding, the sun-god,
The sounds, melodious, falling from his harp,
Recomfort the two worlds, of men and gods.
O'er heaven's wide-shining bent, thou, all day,
　　　speedest,
On fiery wheels, drawn of immortal steeds.
And we, Lord, on thee, call, before all gods,
A lord of flocks; and not to sere our grass.
To midday, come, we pray thee ripe our corn.
And when clothed, angry, in thy purple weed,
Thou battle join'st with the dark welken powers,
Give rain: but us defend, with thy vast targe,
From hail. Come, to the dim world's vaulted brinks,
Where water thy tired steeds, sink thy bright wheels,
Below earth's round, and compass of sea billows:

And seemest thou, then, to die into the night;
Who, daily-born, art eldest of the gods!
But we, on whom, lies spread night's misty murk,
As thou wert dead, then wait, lord, with cold hearts,
And magic chant, beside thine altar-hearths,
Neath stars, thy new uprising, from the East.

THE GAULS SACRIFICE

(*From* The Dawn in Britain)

Now stoops the sun, and dies day's cheerful light.
When stars tread forth, intone this two-tongued folk,
Standing with firebrands, hymns of sacrifice,
Mongst the cold Alps: rebellow whose bleak cliffs'
White flinty bosoms, world's unwonted voice.
Spoiled, the two young men, to their girdle-steads,
(Whose swan-breasts like to ivory images,
Of graven gods!) stand proudly, and do outstretch,
O'er the altar's stone, their necks. Behold then priests,
Carve, with sharp knives of flint, his and his gorge!
Darkened their sense, both loosing blood and breath;
The victims fall; and falling seemed embrace;
Their faces dead, turned towards Italia.

A ROMAN OFFICER WRITES

(*From* The Dawn in Britain)

                 Sempronius,
Sends greeting, warden of this Roman shore.
And be it known, to thee, most excellent Priscus,
According to what certain word we heard;

C. M. DOUGHTY

From mouth of Sequana, lately sailed great vessel,
Called the Bucefalus; which was ship of charge,
With victual, and the year's relief of soldiers.
Dread is; they, in ere-yester's tempest, perished.
Timbers and tables drifted up, all night,
Under my station. Then, at dawning light,
Were weltering carcases seen of legionaries,
In billows heaving: which be drawn to shore,
At my commandment. And I gather wood,
To make drowned soldiers seemly funerals.
Even as I write, is found the body of Faustus,
Captain of soldiers, of the second cohort.
Given at this Roman tower. Pictonia.

    Avert the immortal gods, from us, all evil!
Know, after I had sealed the former scroll,
I sent out barks. Then many, upon sharp skerries,
Left by the ebbing tide, were corses found.
These drawn to shore, bade I then lay, on rows;
Mongst whom, as many doubt, forbid it gods!
A young man lies, like thy son Lepidus,
Who sailed, in that great vessel, the same tide.
Lo, I thee send his ring, for a sure token.
Strengthen thee, in this sorrow, I pray the gods!

KEITH DOUGLAS

DESERT FLOWERS

Living in a wide landscape are the flowers—
Rosenberg I only repeat what you were saying—
the shell and the hawk, every hour
are slaying men and jerboas, slaying

the mind: but the body can fill
the hungry flowers and dogs who cry words
at nights, the most hostile things of all.
But that is not new. Each time the night discards

draperies on the eyes and leaves the mind awake
I look each side of the door of sleep
for the little coin it will take
to buy the secret I shall not keep.

I see men as trees suffering
or confound the detail and the horizon.
Lay the coin on my tongue and I will sing
of what the others never set eyes on.

THE DECEASED

He was a reprobate I grant
and always liquored till his money went.

His hair depended on a noose from
a Corona Veneris. His eyes, dumb

like prisoners in their cavernous slots, were
settled in attitudes of despair.

KEITH DOUGLAS

You who God bless you never sunk so low
censure and pray for him that he was so;

and with his failings you regret the verses
the fellow made, probably between curses,

probably in the extremes of moral decay,
but he wrote them in a sincere way:

and appears to have felt a refined pain
to which your virtue cannot attain.

Respect him. For this
He had an excellence which you miss.

LAWRENCE DURRELL

NEMEA

A song in the valley of Nemea:
Sing quiet, quite quiet here.

Song for the brides of Argos
Combing the swarms of golden hair:
Quite quiet, quiet there.

Under the rolling comb of grass,
The sword outrusts the golden helm.

Agamemnon under tumulus serene
Outsmiles the jury of skeletons:
Cool under cumulus the lion queen:

Only the drum can celebrate,
Only the adjective outlive them.

A song in the valley of Nemea:
Sing quiet, quiet, quiet here.

Tone of the frog in the empty well,
Drone of the bald bee on the cold skull,

Quiet, Quiet, Quiet.

LA FIGLIA CHE PIANGE

O quam te memorem virgo . . .

Stand on the highest pavement of the stair—
Lean on a garden urn—
Weave, weave the sunlight in your hair—
Clasp your flowers to you with a pained surprise—
Fling them to the ground and turn
With a fugitive resentment in your eyes:
But weave, weave the sunlight in your hair.

So I would have had him leave,
So I would have had her stand and grieve,
So he would have left
As the soul leaves the body torn and bruised,
As the mind deserts the body it has used.
I should find
Some way incomparably light and deft,
Some way we both should understand,
Simple and faithless as a smile and shake of the hand.

She turned away, but with the autumn weather
Compelled my imagination many days,
Many days and many hours:
Her hair over her arms and her arms full of flowers.
And I wonder how they should have been together!
I should have lost a gesture and a pose.
Sometimes these cogitations still amaze
The troubled midnight and the noon's repose.

LINES FOR AN OLD MAN

T. S. ELIOT

The tiger in the tiger-pit
Is not more irritable than I.
The whipping tail is not more still
Than when I smell the enemy
Writhing in the essential blood
Or dangling from the friendly tree.
When I lay bare the tooth of wit
The hissing over the arched tongue
Is more affectionate than hate,
More bitter than the love of youth,
And inaccessible by the young.
Reflected from my golden eye
The dullard knows that he is mad.
Tell me if I am not glad!

From LITTLE GIDDING

Ash on an old man's sleeve
Is all the ash the burnt roses leave.
Dust in the air suspended
Marks the place where a story ended.
Dust inbreathed was a house—
The wall, the wainscot and the mouse.
The death of hope and despair,
   This is the death of air.

There are flood and drouth
Over the eyes and in the mouth,
Dead water and dead sand
Contending for the upper hand.
The parched eviscerate soil
Gapes at the vanity of toil,
Laughs without mirth
   This is the death of earth.

T. S. ELIOT

      Water and fire succeed
      The town, the pasture and the weed.
      Water and fire deride
      The sacrifice that we denied.
      Water and fire shall rot
      The marred foundations we forgot,
      Of sanctuary and choir.
          This is the death of water and fire.

In the uncertain hour before the morning
   Near the ending of interminable night
   At the recurrent end of the unending
After the dark dove with the flickering tongue
   Had passed below the horizon of his homing
   While the dead leaves still rattled on like tin
Over the asphalt where no other sound was
   Between three districts whence the smoke arose
   I met one walking, loitering and hurried
As if blown towards me like the metal leaves
   Before the urban dawn wind unresisting
   And as I fixed upon the down-turned face
That pointed scrutiny with which we challenge
   The first-met stranger in the waning dusk
   I caught the sudden look of some dead master
Whom I had known, forgotten, half recalled
   Both one and many; in the brown baked features
   The eyes of a familiar compound ghost
Both intimate and unidentifiable.
   So I assumed a double part, and cried
   And heard another's voice cry: 'What! are *you* here?'
Although we were not. I was still the same,
   Knowing myself yet being someone other—
   And he a face still forming; yet the words sufficed

To compel the recognition they preceded.
    And so, compliant to the common wind,
    Too strange to each other for misunderstanding,
In concord at this intersection time
    Of meeting nowhere, no before and after,
    We trod the pavement in a dead patrol.
I said: 'The wonder that I feel is easy,
    Yet ease is cause of wonder. Therefore speak:
    I may not comprehend, may not remember.'
And he: 'I am not eager to rehearse
    My thought and theory which you have forgotten.
    These things have served their purpose: let them be.
So with your own, and pray they be forgiven
    By others, as I pray you to forgive
    Both bad and good. Last season's fruit is eaten
And the fullfed beast shall kick the empty pail.
    For last year's words belong to last year's language
    And next year's words await another voice.
But, as the passage now presents no hindrance
    To the spirit unappeased and peregrine
    Between two worlds become much like each other,
So I find words I never thought to speak
    In streets I never thought I should revisit
    When I left my body on a distant shore.
Since our concern was speech, and speech impelled us
    To purify the dialect of the tribe
    And urge the mind to aftersight and foresight,
Let me disclose the gifts reserved for age
    To set a crown upon your lifetime's effort.
    First, the cold friction of expiring sense
Without enchantment, offering no promise
    But bitter tastelessness of shadow fruit
    As body and soul begin to fall asunder.
Second, the conscious impotence of rage

T. S. ELIOT

At human folly, and the laceration
Of laughter at what ceases to amuse.
And last, the rending pain of re-enactment
   Of all that you have done, and been; the shame
   Of motives late revealed, and the awareness
Of things ill done and done to others' harm
   Which once you took for exercise of virtue.
   Then fools' approval stings, and honour stains.
From wrong to wrong the exasperated spirit
   Proceeds, unless restored by that refining fire
   Where you must move in measure, like a dancer.'
The day was breaking. In the disfigured street
   He left me, with a kind of valediction,
   And faded on the blowing of the horn.

WILLIAM EMPSON

TO AN OLD LADY

Ripeness is all; her in her cooling planet
Revere; do not presume to think her wasted.
Project her no projectile, plan nor man it;
Gods cool in turn, by the sun long outlasted.

Our earth alone given no name of god
Gives, too, no hold for such a leap to aid her;
Landing you break some palace and seem odd;
Bees sting their need, the keeper's queen invader.

No, to your telescope; spy out the land;
Watch while her ritual is still to see,
Still stand her temples emptying in the sand
Whose waves o'erthrew their crumbled tracery;

Still stand uncalled-on her soul's appanage;
Much social detail whose successor fades,
Wit used to run a house and to play Bridge,
And tragic fervour, to dismiss her maids.

Years her precession do not throw from gear.
She reads a compass certain of her pole;
Confident, finds no confines on her sphere,
Whose failing crops are in her sole control.

Stars how much further from me fill my night,
Strange that she too should be inaccessible,
Who shares my sun. He curtains her from sight,
And but in darkness is she visible.

AUBADE

WILLIAM EMPSON

Hours before dawn we were woken by the quake.
My house was on a cliff. The thing could take
Bookload off shelves, break bottles in a row.
Then the long pause and then the bigger shake.
It seemed the best thing to be up and go.

And far too large for my feet to step by.
I hoped that various buildings were brought low.
The heart of standing is you cannot fly.

It seemed quite safe till she got up and dressed.
The guarded tourist makes the guide the test.
Then I said The Garden? Laughing she said No.
Taxi for her and for me healthy rest.
It seemed the best thing to be up and go.

The language problem but you have to try.
Some solid ground for lying could she show?
The heart of standing is you cannot fly.

None of these deaths were her point at all.
The thing was that being woken he would bawl
And finding her not in earshot he would know.
I tried saying Half an Hour to pay this call.
It seemed the best thing to be up and go.

I slept, and blank as that I would yet lie.
Till you have seen what a threat holds below,
The heart of standing is you cannot fly.

Tell me again about Europe and her pains,
Who's tortured by the drought, who by the rains.
Glut me with floods where only the swine can row
Who cuts his throat and let him count his gains.
It seemed the best thing to be up and go.

A bedshift flight to a Far Eastern sky.　　　　WILLIAM
Only the same war on a stronger toe.　　　　　EMPSON
The heart of standing is you cannot fly.

Tell me more quickly what I lost by this,
Or tell me with less drama what they miss
Who call no die a god for a good throw,
Who say after two aliens had one kiss
It seemed the best thing to be up and go.

But as to risings, I can tell you why.
It is on contradiction that they grow.
It seemed the best thing to be up and go.
Up was the heartening and the strong reply.
The heart of standing is we cannot fly.

ANNE FINCH

From ESSAY ON MARRIAGE

O, love, in your sweet name enough
Illusory pretentious stuff
Is talked and written. Myth and dream
Fix the contemporary scheme
In alien shapes. Can we not make
Some simple statement which will shake
Our valued preconceptions loose;
And, putting to a better use
The innocent and candid sense
Of everyday experience,
Build up a picture of known fact
More subtle, brilliant, and exact?

Tradition is no guide. The old
Romantic impulse has gone cold;
The Christian ethic has in fact
Small bearing on the way we act;
And the inevitable urge
To let a newer style emerge
(Masked by adherence to some creed
We can't believe in, and don't need)
Appears, sporadic and abrupt,
As something formless or corrupt,
Conflicting with the other drives
And broader movement of our lives;
While still an individual past
Weighs on us too, and breeds the last
Infirmity of intellect—
We must achieve what we expect.

JAMES ELROY FLECKER

SANTORIN

(A legend of the Aegean)

'Who are you, Sea Lady,
And where in the seas are we?
I have too long been steering
By the flashes in your eyes.
Why drops the moonlight through my heart,
And why so quietly
Go the great engines of my boat
As if their souls were free?'
'Oh ask me not, bold sailor;
Is not your ship a magic ship
That sails without a sail:
Are not these isles the Isles of Greece
And dust upon the sea?
But answer me three questions
And give me answers three.
What is your ship?' 'A British.'
'And where may Britain be?'
'Oh it lies north, dear lady;
It is a small country.'
'Yet you will know my lover
Though you live far away:
And you will whisper where he has gone,
That lily boy to look upon
And whiter than the spray.'
'How should I know your lover,
Lady of the Sea?'
'Alexander, Alexander,
The King of the World was he.'

JAMES
ELROY
FLECKER

'Weep not for him, dear lady,
But come aboard my ship,
So many years ago he died,
He's dead as dead can be.'
'O base and brutal sailor
To lie this lie to me,
His mother was the foam-foot
Star-sparkling Aphrodite;
His father was Adonis
Who lives away in Lebanon,
In stony Lebanon, where blooms
His red anemone.
But where is Alexander,
The soldier Alexander,
My golden love of olden days
The King of the world and me?'

She sank into the moonlight
And the sea was only sea.

THE PARROT

The old professor of Zoology
Shook his long beard and spake these words to me:
'Compare the Parrot with the Dove. They are
In shape the same: in hue dissimilar.
The Indian bird, which may be sometimes seen
In red or black, is generally green.
His beak is very hard: it has been known
To crack thick nuts and penetrate a stone.
Alas that when you teach him how to speak
You find his head is harder than his beak.

The passionless Malay can safely drub
The pates of parrots with an iron club:
The ingenious fowls, like boys they beat at school,
Soon learn to recognise a Despot's rule.
    Now if you'd train a parrot, catch him young
While soft the mouth and tractable the tongue.
Old birds are fools: they dodder in their speech,
More eager to forget than you to teach;
They swear one curse, then gaze at you askance,
And all oblivion thickens in their glance.

Thrice blest whose parrot of his own accord
Invents new phrases to delight his Lord,
Who spurns the dull quotidian task and tries
Selected words that prove him good and wise.
Ah, once it was my privilege to know
A bird like this . . .
    But that was long ago!'

JAMES
ELROY
FLECKER

DAVID GASCOYNE

AN ELEGY
R.R. 1916–41

Friend, whose unnatural early death
In this year's cold, chaotic Spring
Is like a clumsy wound that will not heal:
What can I say to you, now that your ears
Are stoppered-up with distant soil?
Perhaps to speak at all is false; more true
Simply to sit at times alone and dumb
And with most pure intensity of thought
And concentrated inmost feeling, reach
Towards your shadow on the years' crumbling wall.

I'll say not any word in praise or blame
Of what you ended with the mere turn of a tap;
Nor to explain, deplore nor yet exploit
The latent pathos of your living years—
Hurried, confused and unfulfilled—
That were the shiftless years of both our youths
Spent in the monstrous mountain-shadow of
Catastrophe that chilled you to the bone:
The certain imminence of which always pursued
You from your heritage of fields and sun . . .

I see your face in hostile sunlight, eyes
Wrinkled against its glare, behind the glass
Of a car's windscreen, while you seek to lose
Yourself in swift devouring of white roads
Unwinding across Europe or America;
Taciturn at the wheel, wrapped in a blaze

Of restlessness that no fresh scent can quench;
In cities of brief sojourn that you pass
Through in your quest for respite, heavy drink
Alone enabling you to bear each hotel night.

Sex, Art and Politics: those poor
Expedients! You tried them each in turn,
With the wry inward smile of one resigned
To join in every complicated game
Adults affect to play. Yet girls you found
So prone to sentiment's corruptions; and the joy
Of sensual satisfaction seemed so brief, and left
Only new need. It proved hard to remain
Convinced of the Word's efficacity; or even quite
Certain of World-Salvation through 'the Party
    Line' . . .

Cased in the careful armour that you wore
Of wit and nonchalance, through which
Few quizzed the concealed countenance of fear,
You waited daily for the sky to fall;
At moments wholly panic-stricken by
A sense of stifling in your brittle shell;
Seeing the world's damnation week by week
Grow more and more inevitable; till
The conflagration broke out with a roar,
And from those flames you fled through whirling
    smoke,

To end at last in bankrupt exile in
That sordid city, scene of *Ulysses*; and there,
While War sowed all the lands with violent graves,
You finally succumbed to a black, wild
Incomprehensibility of fate that none could share . . .
Yet even in your obscure death I see

DAVID The secret candour of that lonely child
GAS- Who, lost in the storm-shaken castle-park,
COYNE Astride his crippled mastiff's back was borne
      Slowly away into the utmost dark.

ORPHEUS IN THE UNDERWORLD

Curtains of rock
And tears of stone,
Wet leaves in a high crevice of the sky:
From side to side the draperies
Drawn back by rigid hands.

And he came carrying the shattered lyre,
And wearing the blue robes of a king.
And looking through eyes like holes torn in a screen;
And the distant sea was faintly heard,
From time to time, in the suddenly rising wind,
Like a broken song.

Out of his sleep, from time to time,
From between half open lips,
Escaped the bewildered words which try to tell
The tale of his bright night
And his wing-shadowed day
The soaring flights of thought beneath the sun
Above the islands of the seas
And all the deserts, all the pastures, all the plains
Of the distracting foreign land.

He sleeps with the broken lyre between his hands,
And round his slumber are drawn back
The rigid draperies, the tears and wet leaves,
Cold curtains of rock concealing the bottomless sky.

THE SACRED HEARTH

DAVID GASCOYNE

To George Barker

You must have been still sleeping, your wife there
Asleep beside you. All the old oak breathed: while slow,
How slow the intimate Spring night swelled through those depths
Of soundlessness and dew-chill shadow on towards the day.
Yet I, alone awake close by, was summoned suddenly
By distant voice more indistinct though more distinctly clear,
While all inaudible, than any dream's, calling on me to rise
And stumble barefoot down the stairs to seek the air
Outdoors, so sweet and somnolent, not cold, and at that hour
Suspending in its glass undrifting milk-strata of mist,
Stilled by the placid beaming of the adolescent moon.
There, blackly outlined in their moss-green light, they stood,
The trees of the small crabbed and weed-grown orchard,
Perfect as part of one of Calvert's idylls. It was then,
Wondering what calm magnet had thus drawn me from my bed,
I wandered out across the briar-bound garden, spellbound. Most
Mysterious and unrecapturable moment, when I stood
There staring back at the dark white nocturnal house,
And saw gleam through the lattice a light more pure than gold

DAVID GASCOYNE Made sanguine with crushed roses, from the firelight that all night
Stayed flickering about the sacred hearth. As long as dawn
Hung fire behind the branch-hid sky, the strong
Magic of rustic slumber held unbroken; yet a song
Sprang wordlessly from inertia in my heart, to see how near
A neighbour strangeness ever stands to home. George, in the wood
Of wandering among wood-hiding trees, where poet's art
Is how to whistle in the dark, where pockets all have holes,
All roofs for refugees have rents, we ought to know
That there can be for us no place quite alien and unknown,
No situation wholly hostile, if somewhere there burn
The faithful fire of vision still awaiting our return.

WILFRID GIBSON

HENRY TURNBULL

He planked down sixpence and he took his drink;
Then slowly picked the change up from the zinc,
And in his breeches-pocket buttoned tight
Two greasy pennies, which that very night
Were used by Betty Catchieside, called in
To lay him out, when she'd tied up his chin,
To keep his eyelids shut: and so he lies
With tuppence change till Doomsday on his eyes.

TO MY FATHER

Yes as alike as entirely
You my father I see
That high Greenock tenement
And whole shipyarded front.

As alike as a memory early
Of 'The Bonny Earl o' Moray'
Fiddled in our high kitchen
Over the sleeping town

These words this one night
Feed us and will not
Leave us without our natures
Inheriting new fires.

The March whinfires let fall
From the high Greenock hill
A word fetched so bright
Out of the forehead that

A fraction's wink and I
And my death change round softly.
My birth and I so softly
Change round the outward journey.

Entirely within the fires
And winter-harried natures
Of your each year, the still
Foundered man is the oracle

Tented within his early
Friendships. And he'll reply
To us locked in our song.
This night this word falling

Across the kindling skies
Takes over over our bodies.

W. S.
GRAHAM

THE CHILDREN OF GREENOCK

Local I'll bright my tale on, how
She rose up white on a Greenock day
Like the one first-of-all morning
On earth, and heard children singing.

She in a listening shape stood still
In a high tenement at Spring's sill
Over the street and chalked lawland
Peevered and lined and fancymanned

On a pavement shouting games and faces.
She saw them children of all cries
With everyone's name against them bled
In already the helpless world's bed.

Already above the early town
The smoky government was blown
To cover April. The local orient's
Donkeymen, winches and steel giants

Wound on the sugar docks. Clydeside,
Webbed in its foundries and loud blood,
Binds up the children's cries alive.
Her own red door kept its young native.

W. S.
GRAHAM

Her own window by several sights
Wept and became the shouting streets.
And her window by several sights
Adored the even louder seedbeats.

She leaned at the bright mantle brass
Fairly a mirror of surrounding sorrows,
The sown outcome of always war
Against the wordperfect, public tear.

Brighter drifted upon her the sweet sun
High already over all the children
So chained and happy in Cartsburn Street
Barefoot on authority's alphabet.

Her window watched the woven care
Hang webbed within the branched and heavy
Body. It watched the blind unborn
Copy book after book of sudden

Elements within the morning of her
Own man-locked womb. It saw the neighbour
Fear them housed in her walls of blood.
It saw two towns, but a common brood.

Her window watched the shipyards sail
Their men away. The sparrow sill
Bent grey over the struck town clocks
Striking two towns, and fed its flocks.

LISTEN. PUT ON MORNING

W. S. GRAHAM

Listen. Put on morning.
Waken into falling light.
A man's imagining
Suddenly may inherit
The handclapping centuries
Of his one minute on earth.
And hear the virgin juries
Talk with his own breath
To the corner boys of his street.
And hear the Black Maria
Searching the town at night.
And hear the playropes caa
The sister Mary in.
And hear Willie and Davie
Among the bracken of Narnain
Sing in a mist heavy
With myrtle and listeners.
And hear the higher town
Weep a petition of fears
At the poorhouse close upon
The public heartbeat.
And hear the children tig
And run with my own feet
Into the netting drag
Of a suiciding principle.
Listen. Put on lightbreak.
Waken into miracle.
The audience lies awake
Under the tenements
Under the sugar docks
Under the printed moments.
The centuries turn their locks
And open under the hill

W. S. GRAHAM

Their inherited books and doors
All gathered to distil
Like happy berry pickers
One voice to talk to us.
Yes listen. It carries away
The second and the years
Till the heart's in a jacket of snow
And the head's in a helmet white
And the song sleeps to be wakened
By the morning ear bright.
Listen. Put on morning.
Waken into falling light.

THE NAME LIKE A RIVER

The gean trees drive me to love
To the landwave wearing the shipwreck down
To observing flint-seed through seesaw eyes
From my loss of level in the to-fro bone.
Not resting I look by my seas
In each twin lovewave eye at the gowan
Where over summer the spinning turnstiles
Flower the girl from the green-dyked town.

Let nothing through love's way leave
But the ringing through hawthorn disciple's name
That ever by my bellstrong mouth I scold
On the grindwheel gale that draws me to calm.
Let the young of her tasted and tongued
Ear bite on the voice of her knuckled alarum
Making loud the wrecked lad on her rippling
    door
Making sure and sharing the lad I am.

W. S. GRAHAM

The shoremark draws me through love
As drew the womanlaid deadman under
The lettering sand that she walks and reads.
With five seas down the arm-clenched air
Speaks over the skidding seaskin
The picture of ballast and the bunched water.
The load I fling from the bird-perched ben
Young climbs the sand-laid warrior.

This voice is nothing yet holding
Where love is all ash, a pasture for stone
A wreck for the spar-honing breath to dress
With red at the lips, with red on the fin
In the seesaw scupper beds.
The shore aslant as the host comes in
Lets nothing through love's way but words
Bird-printed, sharing the lad I am.

The buttercups drive me to love
Yet the sea on the atlas-sided boulder
Wrecks many a blood-dressed stem.
The comeback prow yet holding flower
Crows through the weather's barrack
The true disciple's name like a river.
The womanlaid drives me to love
With the brightshaped wreck of love on my
      shoulder.

A LOVE STORY

The full moon easterly rising, furious,
Against a winter sky ragged with red;
The hedges high in snow, and owls raving—
Solemnities not easy to withstand:
A shiver wakes the spine.

In boyhood, having encountered the scene,
I suffered horror: I fetched the moon home,
With owls and snow, to nurse in my head
Throughout the trials of a new spring,
Famine unassuaged.

But fell in love, and made a lodgement
Of love on those chill ramparts.
Her image was my ensign: snows melted,
Hedges sprouted, the moon tenderly shone,
The owls trilled with tongues of nightingale.

These were all lies, though they matched the time,
And brought me less than luck: her image
Warped in the weather, turned beldamish.
Then back came winter on me at a bound,
The pallid sky heaved with a moon-quake.

Dangerous it had been with love-notes
To serenade Queen Famine.
In tears I recomposed the former scene,
Let the snow lie, watched the moon rise, suffered the
    owls,
Paid homage to them of unevent.

THE LAUREATE

ROBERT GRAVES

Like a lizard in the sun, though not scuttling
When men approach, this wretch, this thing of rage,
Scowls and sits rhyming in his horny age.

His time and truth he has not bridged to ours,
But shrivelled by long heliotropic idling
He croaks at us his out-of-date humours.

Once long ago here was a poet; who died.
See how remorse twitching his mouth proclaims
It was no natural death, but suicide.

Arrogant, lean, unvenerable, he
Still turns for comfort to the western flames
That glitter a cold span above the sea.

ULYSSES

To the much-tossed Ulysses, never done
    With woman whether gowned as wife or whore,
Penelope and Circe seemed as one:
She like a whore made his lewd fancies run,
    And wifely she a hero to him bore.

Their counter-changings terrified his way:
    They were the clashing rocks, Symplegades,
Scylla and Charybdis too were they;
Now they were storms frosting the sea with spray
    And now the lotus island's drunken ease.

They multiplied into the Sirens' throng,
    Forewarned by fear of whom he stood bound fast

ROBERT GRAVES Hand and foot helpless to the vessel's mast,
Yet would not stop his ears: daring their song
    He groaned and sweated till that shore was past.

One, two and many: flesh had made him blind,
    Flesh had one pleasure only in the act,
Flesh set one purpose only in the mind—
Triumph of flesh and afterwards to find
    Still those same terrors wherewith flesh was racked.

His wiles were witty and his fame far known,
Every king's daughter sought him for her own,
    Yet he was nothing to be won or lost.
    All lands to him were Ithaca: love-tossed
He loathed the fraud, yet would not bed alone.

SHE TELLS HER LOVE WHILE HALF ASLEEP

She tells her love while half asleep,
    In the dark hours,
        With half-words whispered low:
As Earth stirs in her winter sleep
    And puts out grass and flowers
        Despite the snow,
        Despite the falling snow.

DOWN, WANTON, DOWN!

Down, wanton, down! Have you no shame
That at the whisper of Love's name,
Or Beauty's, presto! up you raise
Your angry head and stand at gaze?

Poor bombard-captain, sworn to reach
The ravelin and effect a breach—
Indifferent what you storm or why,
So be that in the breach you die!

Love may be blind, but Love at least
Knows what is man and what mere beast;
Or Beauty wayward, but requires
More delicacy from her squires.

Tell me, my witless, whose one boast
Could be your staunchness at the post,
When were you made a man of parts
To think fine and profess the arts?

Will many-gifted Beauty come
Bowing to your bald rule of thumb,
Or Love swear loyalty to your crown?
Be gone, have done! Down, wanton, down!

NATURE'S LINEAMENTS

When mountain rocks and leafy trees
And clouds and things like these,
With edges,

Caricature the human face,
Such scribblings have no grace
Or peace—

The bulbous nose, the sunken chin,
The ragged mouth in grin
Of cretin.

ROBERT GRAVES

Nature is always so: you find
That all it has of mind
Is wind,

Retching among the empty spaces,
Ruffling the idiot grasses,
The sheep's fleeces.

Whose pleasures are excreting, poking,
Havocking and sucking,
Sleepy licking.

Whose griefs are melancholy,
Whose flowers are oafish,
Whose waters, silly,
Whose birds, raffish,
Whose fish, fish.

LAMENT FOR PASIPHAE

Dying sun, shine warm a little longer!
My eye, dazzled with tears, shall dazzle yours,
Conjuring you to shine and not to move.
You, sun, and I all afternoon have laboured
Beneath a dewless and oppressive cloud—
A fleece now gilded with our common grief
That this must be a night without a moon.
Dying sun, shine warm a little longer!

Faithless she was not: she was very woman,
Smiling with dire impartiality,
Sovereign, with heart unmatched, adored of men,
Until Spring's cuckoo with bedraggled plumes
Tempted her pity and her truth betrayed.
Then she who shone for all resigned her being,
And this must be a night without a moon.
Dying sun, shine warm a little longer!

THOM GUNN

TAMER AND HAWK

I thought I was so tough,
But gentled at your hands
Cannot be quick enough
To fly for you and show
That when I go I go
At your commands.

Even in flight above
I am no longer free:
You seeled me with your love,
I am blind to other birds—
The habit of your words
Has hooded me.

As formerly, I wheel
I hover and I twist,
But only want the feel,
In my possessive thought,
Of catcher and of caught
Upon your wrist.

You but half-civilize,
Taming me in this way.
Through having only eyes
For you I fear to lose,
I lose to keep, and choose
Tamer as prey.

A CHURCH ROMANCE

(*Mellstock: circa* 1835)

She turned in the high pew, until her sight
Swept the west gallery, and caught its row
Of music-men with viol, book, and bow
Against the sinking sad tower-window light.

She turned again; and in her pride's despite
One strenuous viol's inspirer seemed to throw
A message from his string to her below,
Which said: 'I claim thee as my own forthright!'

Thus their hearts' bond began, in due time signed.
And long years thence, when Age had scared
    Romance,
At some old attitude of his or glance
That gallery-scene would break upon her mind,
With him as minstrel, ardent, young, and trim,
Bowing 'New Sabbath' or 'Mount Ephraim'.

LAUSANNE

IN GIBBON'S OLD GARDEN: 11–12 p.m.
June 27, 1897

(*The* 110*th anniversary of the completion of the 'Decline and Fall' at the same hour and place*)

  A spirit seems to pass,
 Formal in pose, but grave withal and grand:
 He contemplates a volume in his hand,
And far lamps fleck him through the thin acacias.

   Anon the book is closed,
  With 'It is finished!' And at the alley's end
  He turns, and when on me his glances bend
As from the Past comes speech—small, muted, yet
    composed.

   'How fares the Truth now?—Ill?
  —Do pens but slily further her advance?
  May one not speed her but in phrase askance?
Do scribes aver the Comic to be Reverend still?

   'Still rule those minds on earth
  At whom sage Milton's wormwood words were
    hurled:
  "Truth like a bastard comes into the world
Never without ill-fame to him who gives her birth"?'

TESS'S LAMENT

I would that folk forgot me quite,
                Forgot me quite!
I would that I could shrink from sight,
    And no more see the sun.
Would it were time to say farewell,
To claim my nook, to need my knell,
Time for them all to stand and tell,
    Of my day's work as done.

Ah! dairy where I lived so long,
                I lived so long;
Where I would rise up staunch and strong,
    And lie down hopefully.
'Twas there within the chimney-seat
He watched me to the clock's slow beat—
Loved me, and learnt to call me Sweet,
    And whispered words to me.

THOMAS HARDY

And now he's gone; and now he's gone; . . .
                And now he's gone!
The flowers we potted perhaps are thrown
    To rot upon the farm.
And where we had our supper-fire
May now grow nettle, dock, and briar,
And all the place be mould and mire
    So cozy once and warm.

And it was I who did it all,
                Who did it all;
'Twas I who made the blow to fall
    On him who thought no guile.
Well, it is finished—past, and he
Has left me to my misery,
And I must take my Cross on me
    For wronging him awhile.

How gay we looked that day we wed,
                That day we wed!
'May joy be with ye!' they all said
    A-standing by the durn.
I wonder what they say o' us now,
And if they know my lot; and how
She feels who milks my favourite cow,
    And takes my place at churn!

It wears me out to think of it,
                To think of it;
I cannot bear my fate as writ,
    I'd have my life unbe;
Would turn my memory to a blot,
Make every relic of me rot,
My doings be as they were not,
    And gone all trace of me!

THE CONVERGENCE OF THE TWAIN

THOMAS HARDY

(*Lines on the loss of the 'Titanic'*)

    In a solitude of the sea
    Deep from human vanity,
And the Pride of Life that planned her, stilly couches she.

    Steel chambers, late the pyres
    Of her salamandrine fires,
Cold currents thrid, and turn to rhythmic tidal lyres.

    Over the mirrors meant
    To glass the opulent
The sea-worm crawls—grotesque, slimed, dumb, indifferent.

    Jewels in joy designed
    To ravish the sensuous mind
Lie lightless, all their sparkles bleared and black and blind.

    Dim moon-eyed fishes near
    Gaze at the gilded gear
And query: 'What does this vaingloriousness down here?' . . .

    Well: while was fashioning
    This creature of cleaving wing,
The Immanent Will that stirs and urges everything

    Prepared a sinister mate
    For her—so gaily great—
A Shape of Ice, for the time far and dissociate.

THOMAS
HARDY
   And as the smart ship grew
    In stature, grace, and hue,
In shadowy silent distance grew the Iceberg too.

    Alien they seemed to be:
    No mortal eye could see
The intimate welding of their later history,

    Or sign that they were bent
    By paths coincident
On being anon twin halves of one august event,

    Till the Spinner of the Years
    Said 'Now!' And each one hears,
And consummation comes, and jars two hemispheres.

I LOOK INTO MY GLASS

I look into my glass,
And view my wasting skin,
And say, 'Would God it came to pass
My heart had shrunk as thin!'

For then, I, undistrest
By hearts grown cold to me,
Could lonely wait my endless rest
With equanimity.

But Time, to make me grieve,
Part steals, lets part abide;
And shakes this fragile frame at eve
With throbbings of noontide.

THOMAS HENNELL

QUEEN ANNE'S MUSICIANS

Poor Doctor Blow went out of church
Death-struck ere sermon ended—
With staggering tread he's seen to lurch:
Six ermined quiresmen stand aside,
But he's by none befriended.
Lights flicker out at organ-perch;
' 'Twas time he died,' the people sighed,
'By apoplexy struck, 'tis clear he's done for.'

   The fiddlers, in a wainscot room,
Strike rounds upon the strings:
But quakes the floor, and shiv'ring doom
Upsets their quaverings . . .
Their chorus half-way stuck, no door's to run for.

   Purcell within stone-vaulted abbey
Played pipes or virginals:
The thin-drawn notes re-echoed late
And sounded back from loft and walls.
   Yet now wax quaint and shabby
As chamber-mated pewter spoons
Old tinkling tunes, which creak and grate.
Fate's left instead of luck: what's candle lit in sun for?

SHEPHERD AND SHEPHERDESS

    O for our upland meads,
    Wherein of childhood's deeds
    To prattle, fancy leads
    Past rills, and groves of trees.

THOMAS HENNELL

For camomile and orchis,
Fritillary, our search is,
A wreath that lovers purchase
With a sweet kiss in the eyes.

By shade of ash and laurels
We will forget our quarrels,
Sourer than August sorrels
Nibbled with bread and cheese.

Kerchiefed tomatoes red
Here on a hillock spread:
Fetch water from the stream,
That fancy here may dream.

Pleasures so kind as these
The silly minutes please,
Our flocks, upon the leas
May scatter far as wandering bees.

A MERMAIDEN

Cast up on the Cornish coast (as reported), Sept. 1934

Chilled with salt dew, tossed on dark waters deep,
Sailors and fishers loved her in their sleep,
And not a few would wed her in their dreams!
   Yet when, within their net, one autumn night
They felt and dragged her sliding weight, it seems
Star-sprinkled skies and phosphorescent light
On all the billows' tops, and on the net
Making a spider's-mesh of sparkles bright,
Dripping like pearls off her curled horse-tail hair—
Low-breathed they haul, and dunch! she's on the
      planks all right.

What may be done with her can no man fathom, yet THOMAS
Pretty as paint she starts, but tails so awkwardly. HENNELL
Nor any of the crew will wish or dare
To take her home and, for their very lives,
To face again their daughters and their wives.

   No fishing-clouts will fit her quite, and all in vain
They put her out fried mackerel and hot tea.
Says one, 'Things being a turn of year
'We'll take ashore the maid, and at the church
'Of Lanteglos-by-Fowey, being near—
'Along with pilchards, breams, and perch,
'Fruit, turnips, autumn-flowers and marrows
'Which ornament the choir-stalls, piers, and rails
'And openings of pulpit narrow,
'Put her in window for the Harvest Show!'
   '—Though folk will have to mind her dripping tails
'Upon their bonnets, hymn-books, shawls, and pews.
'I'll hurry to the Rector with the news,
'And just remark, "Look here, sir, what we've found!
' "Are we to drop her back, or in a tank
' "Send her along to the Aquarium?" '
'O-ho!' some others cried,
'We'll run her up the High-Street in a barrow.'

   An elder stroked his chin, and drank some rum
From wickered bottle: 'Nay, for did we so,
'Being a witch, she'd visit us with woe;
'Or nightmares foul, or other sort of itch—
'She, or some kindred doubtful spirit dumb!
'—She weeps, and calls her lover, but in vain,
'These sea-maids marry none but sailors drowned,
'Fetch wind-spouts, or bring whirlpools in a calm!'
   With this, he smites one crab-fist down in palm,
'I'll just say what, we'll simply scrag the witch!

Thomas   'And in the cauldron used for melting pitch
Hennell 'Boil down the tail-end: she is every sailor's foe
'And simply lures poor duffers to their fate.
'The rest we'll cut in lumps and use for bait.'

'On this, the boatswain rather sternly spoke:
'Friend, what you say goes farther than a joke.
' 'Twas honest counsel beyond any doubt,
'Yet did the parish constable find out,
'He and the clergyman would call it guilt:
'So might for her cold blood thy hot be spilt!'

So then a more religious gave his mind:
' 'Twould be temptation to the village boys
'And frighten half the maids, if they should find
'That ladies such as this should be.
'Who may betroth the dead, or with a spirit
'Vex us, and what our children may inherit:
'And bring about, perhaps, our total loss.
'We, being Christians, needs must sink her with the
        cross.'

And so with spars and ropes they made her fast
And with the anchor sank. There, fathoms deep,
She found the sandy bottom, so for aye to sleep.

Later near by they hung a passing bell
Hard by a charted rock: which tolls the rising swell.

RAYNER HEPPENSTALL

ACTAEON

This legend is told of me,
That having enjoyed with eyes only
The body no man might know of Artemis
I was translated
Both of substance and of attributes
And seeming to them the vulnerable stag
Torn asunder by dogs my own hands had fed.

Know then that the Lady Artemis
Rested a long night through on my couch, in my arms,
But such is the vehement smiling of her flesh,
She stays unknown of man, she has achieved
That most hateful violation of flesh
Which is to enjoy and be inviolate,
And I her partner in this occult sin,
Seeming I know not what to these bland faces,
Am endlessly torn by dogs in my own flesh seeded.

BAEDEKER FOR METAPHYSICIANS

Having written several poems which I will not publish
And having on my hands two problems which I do not relish
I find literature is a side issue to survival
But, having survived, will that obtain my arrival
At the courts of peace? I suspect I travel with broken gears
Over a country which was not made for this journey
For it seems that we drive on sex or money
And unless these are properly articulated together
One does not call a sunny day good weather
And if the parts that relate to them are stolen from the store
You might survive alright, but what for?
Though you look on mountains and rivers and such marvels
And take a child with you on your travels
You might not find this observance or natural creation
Sufficient. And you will not get consolation
Offering lifts to those who have other secrets
And seem to be travelling, you would say, without cheating.
You will not obtain the solution by holding a meeting
To swop travelling advantages that cannot be pooled
It is essential to arrive when you travel, then you will
See, when you have stopped, that the journey is completed.

THE ENTICEMENTS OF VIRTUE

BRIAN HIGGINS

First:
The protracted fever
Second:
The nearly certain
Solvency of September.
Third:
To hold correctly
A valid anarchistic position.
Fourth:
To fill in with exact fitting
Which is equivalent to a perfect excision,
The time spent placating the committee.

And the fifth enticement to which we are all victims,
Is to be the clear spokesman of vicious, honest dictums.

These are the enticements, the allures, the raptures
Which virtue proffers
And with these she captures
Many takers (each sags as he suffers)
O liberal virtue with the modern spice
O safety served with condiment of vice.

ALL OTHER MEN

All other men cower within their deeds
But you present yourself and you are vile,
Warts and all, simple and nerve-shaken
A scrofulous agony embodied in your style.
All is dethroned, the very air is beaten
Offending by not offering offence
Demoting most where you say you most sweeten
And acting by the commonest of sense.

Brian Higgins

All other men, when the final point is pressed
Hedge at the title to the air they breathe
But you belch out the great gulps you have taken
And lay claim to the badness we perceive
In you, as though that were your title
As though it were a virtuous recompense
To grieve a lot because you do so little
Inhabiting the stinking present tense.

GEOFFREY HILL

THE TURTLE DOVE

Love that drained her drained him she'd loved, though
 each
For the other's sake forged passion upon speech,
Bore their close days through sufferance towards night
Where she at length grasped sleep and he lay quiet

As though needing no questions, now, to guess
What her secreting heart could not well hide.
Her caught face flinched in half-sleep at his side.
Yet she, by day, modelled her real distress,

Poised, turned her cheek to the attending world
Of children and intriguers and the old,
Conversed freely, exercised, was admired,
Being strong to dazzle. All this she endured

To affront him. He watched her rough grief work
Under the formed surface of habit. She spoke
Like one long undeceived but she was hurt.
She denied more love, yet her starved eyes caught

His, devouring, at times. Then, as one self-dared,
She went to him, plied there; like a furious dove
Bore down with visitations of such love
As his lithe, fathoming heart absorbed and buried.

GEOFFREY HILL

ASMODEUS

I

They, after the slow building of the house,
Furnished it; brought warmth under the skin.
Tiles, that a year's rough wind could rattle loose,
Being close-pressed still kept storms out and storms in.
(Of all primed and vain citadels, to choose
This, to choose this of all times to begin!)
Acknowledging, they said, one who pursues
Hobbies of serious lust and indoor sin,
Clearly they both stood, lovers without fear,
Might toy with fire brought dangerously to hand
To tame, not exorcise, spirits; though the air
Whistled abstracted menace, could confound
Strength by device, by music reaching the ear,
Lightning conducted forcibly to the ground.

II

The night, then; bravely stiffen; you are one
Whom stars could burn more deeply than the sun,
Guide-book martyr. You, doubtless, hear wings,
Too sheer for cover, swift; the scattered noise
Of darkness looming with propitious things;
And nests of rumour clustered in the world.
So drummed, so shadowed, your mere trudging voice
Might rave at large while easy truths were told,
Bad perjurable stuff, to be forgiven
Because of this lame journey out of mind.
A tax on men to seventy-times-seven,
A busy vigilance of goose and hound,
Keeps up all guards. Since you are outside, go,
Closing the doors of the house and the head also.

RALPH HODGSON

THE HOUSE ACROSS THE WAY

The leaves looked in at the window
Of the house across the way,
At a man that had sinned like you and me
And all poor human clay.
He muttered: 'In a gambol
I took my soul astray.

But tomorrow I'll drag it back from danger,
In the morning, come what may;
For no man knows what season
He shall go his ghostly way.'
And his face fell down upon the table,
And where it fell it lay.

And the wind blew under the carpet
And it said, or it seemed to say:
'Truly, all men must go a-ghosting
And no man knows his day.'
And the leaves stared in at the window
Like people at a play.

From FLYING SCROLLS

THE SNAIL

You never heard a snail in song?
Wait till the first thrush comes along.

*

'Age, age,' groaned the hour-old midge,
'Can't do the twirls I did.'

*

RALPH HODGSON

Dust thou Art, but dust carefully.

*

The Movement, she explained, would bring poetry to the rich.

A. E. HOUSMAN

IN VALLEYS GREEN AND STILL

In valleys green and still
    Where lovers wander maying
They hear from over hill
    A music playing.

Behind the drum and fife,
    Past hawthornwood and hollow,
Through earth and out of life
    The soldiers follow.

The soldier's is the trade:
    In any wind or weather
He steals the heart of maid
    And man together.

The lover and his lass
    Beneath the hawthorn lying
Have heard the soldiers pass,
    And both are sighing.

And down the distance they
    With dying note and swelling
Walk the resounding way
    To the still dwelling.

OH WHO IS THAT YOUNG SINNER

A. E. HOUSMAN

Oh who is that young sinner with the handcuffs on his wrists?
And what has he been after that they groan and shake their fists?
And wherefore is he wearing such a conscience-stricken air?
Oh they're taking him to prison for the colour of his hair.

'Tis a shame to human nature, such a head of hair as his;
In the good old time 'twas hanging for the colour that it is;
Though hanging isn't bad enough and flaying would be fair
For the nameless and abominable colour of his hair.

Oh a deal of pains he's taken and a pretty price he's paid
To hide his poll or dye it of a mentionable shade;
But they've pulled the beggar's hat off for the world to see and stare,
And they're taking him to justice for the colour of his hair.

Now 'tis oakum for his fingers and the treadmill for his feet,
And the quarry-gang of Portland in the cold and in the heat,
And between his spells of labour in the time he has to spare
He can curse the God that made him for the colour of his hair.

HER STRONG ENCHANTMENTS FAILING

A. E. Housman

Her strong enchantments failing,
    Her towers of fear in wreck,
Her limbecks dried of poisons
    And the knife at her neck,

The Queen of air and darkness
    Begins to shrill and cry,
'O young man, O my slayer,
    To-morrow you shall die.'

O Queen of air and darkness,
    I think 'tis truth you say,
And I shall die to-morrow;
    But you will die to-day.

THE WELSH MARCHES

High the vanes of Shrewsbury gleam
Islanded in Severn stream;
The bridges from the steepled crest
Cross the water east and west.

The flag of morn in conqueror's state
Enters at the English gate:
The vanquished eve, as night prevails,
Bleeds upon the road to Wales.

Ages since the vanquished bled
Round my mother's marriage-bed;
There the ravens feasted far
About the open house of war:

A. E. HOUSMAN

When Severn down to Buildwas ran
Coloured with the death of man,
Couched upon her brother's grave
The Saxon got me on the slave.

The sound of fight is silent long
That began the ancient wrong;
Long the voice of tears is still
That wept of old the endless ill.

In my heart it has not died,
The war that sleeps on Severn side;
They cease not fighting, east and west,
On the marches of my breast.

Here the truceless armies yet
Trample, rolled in blood and sweat;
They kill and kill and never die;
And I think that each is I.

None will part us, none undo
The knot that makes one flesh of two,
Sick with hatred, sick with pain,
Strangling—When shall we be slain?

When shall I be dead and rid
Of the wrong my father did?
How long, how long, till spade and hearse
Put to sleep my mother's curse?

TED HUGHES

THE LAKE

Better disguised than the leaf-insect,

A sort of subtler armadillo,
The lake turns with me as I walk.

Snuffles at my feet for what I might drop or kick up,
Sucks and slobbers the stones, snorts through its lips

Into broken glass, smacks its chops.
It has eaten several my size

Without developing a preference—
Prompt, with a splash, to whatever I offer.

It ruffles in its wallow or lies sunning,
Digesting old senseless bicycles

And a few shoes. The fish down there
Do not know they have been swallowed

Any more than the girl out there, who over the stern
    of a rowboat
Tests its depth with her reflection.

Yet how the outlet fears it!—dragging it out,
Black and yellow, a maniac eel,

Battering it to death with sticks and stones.

DAVID JONES

From THE ANATHEMATA

Ship's master:
>before him, in the waist and before it
>>the darling men.

Cheerily, cheerily
>with land to leeward

known-land, known-shore, home-shore
home-light.
>>Cheerly, cheerly men

'gin to work the ropes.
And she bears up for it
>riding her turning shadow.

The incurving *aphlaston* lanterns high above him
behind him
>the plank-built walls converge

to apse his leaning nave.
To his left elbow
>the helmsman

is quite immobile now
>by whose stanced feet

coiled on the drying hemp-coil
>with one eye open

the still ship's cat
>tillers, just perceptibly

her tip of tail.
He inclines himself out-board
>and to her-ward.[1]

The old padrone
>the ancient staggerer
>the vine-juice skipper.

---

[1] i.e. toward the figure of Athene above the harbour to starboard.

What little's left   DAVID
              in the heel of his calix   JONES
asperging the free-board
              to mingle the dead of the wake.
Pious, eld, bright-eyed
             marinus.
Diocesan of us.
             In the deeps of the drink
his precious dregs
             laid up to the gods.
Libation darks her sea.
He would berth us
             to schedule.

THE HOLY OFFICE

Myself unto myself will give
This name, Katharsis-Purgative.
I, who dishevelled ways forsook
To hold the poets' grammar-book,
Bringing to tavern and to brothel
The mind of witty Aristotle,
Lest bards in the attempt should err
Must here be my interpreter:
Wherefore receive now from my lip
Peripatetic scholarship.
To enter heaven, travel hell,
Be piteous or terrible
One positively needs the ease
Of plenary indulgences.
For every true-born mysticist
A Dante is, unprejudiced,
Who safe at ingle-nook, by proxy,
Hazards extremes of heterodoxy,
Like him who finds joy at a table
Pondering the uncomfortable.
Ruling one's life by common sense
How can one fail to be intense?
But I must not accounted be
One of that mumming company—
With him who hies him to appease
His giddy dames' frivolities
While they console him when he whinges
With gold-embroidered Celtic fringes—
Or him who sober all the day
Mixes a naggin in his play—

Or him whose conduct 'seems to own'
His preference for a man of 'tone'—
Or him who plays the ragged patch
To millionaires in Hazelpatch
But weeping after holy fast
Confesses all his pagan past—
Or him who will his hat unfix
Neither to malt nor crucifix
But show to all that poor-dressed be
His high Castilian courtesy—
Or him who loves his Master dear—
Or him who drinks his pint in fear—
Or him who once when snug abed
Saw Jesus Christ without his head
And tried so hard to win for us
The long-lost works of Aeschylus.
But all these men of whom I speak
Make me the sewer of their clique.
That they may dream their dreamy dreams
I carry off their filthy streams
For I can do those things for them
Through which I lost my diadem,
Those things for which Grandmother Church
Left me severely in the lurch.
Thus I relieve their timid arses,
Perform my office of Katharsis.
My scarlet leaves them white as wool:
Through me they purge a bellyful.
To sister mummers one and all
I act as vicar-general
And for each maiden, shy and nervous,
I do a similar kind service.
For I detect without surprise
That shadowy beauty in her eyes,
The 'dare not' of sweet maidenhood

JAMES JOYCE	That answers my corruptive 'would'.
	Whenever publicly we meet

She never seems to think of it;
At night when close in bed she lies
And feels my hand between her thighs
My little love in light attire
Knows the soft flame that is desire.
But Mammon places under ban
The uses of Leviathan
And that high spirit ever wars
On Mammon's countless servitors
Nor can they ever be exempt
From his taxation of contempt.
So distantly I turn to view
The shamblings of that motley crew,
Those souls that hate the strength that mine has
Steeled in the school of old Aquinas.
Where they have crouched and crawled and prayed
I stand, the self-doomed, unafraid,
Unfellowed, friendless and alone,
Indifferent as the herring-bone,
Firm as the mountain-ridges where
I flash my antlers on the air.
Let them continue as is meet
To adequate the balance-sheet.
Though they may labour to the grave
My spirit shall they never have
Nor make my soul with theirs as one
Till the Mahamanvantara be done:
And though they spurn me from their door
My soul shall spurn them evermore.

PATRICK KAVANAGH

SHANCODUFF

My black hills have never seen the sun rising,
Eternally they look north towards Armagh.
Lot's wife would not be salt if she had been
Incurious as my black hills that are happy
When dawn whitens Glassdrummond chapel.

My hills hoard the bright shillings of March
While the sun searches in every pocket.
They are my Alps and I have climbed the Matterhorn
With a sheaf of hay for three perishing calves
In the field under the Big Forth of Rocksavage.

The sleety winds fondle the rushy beards of Shancoduff
While the cattle-drovers sheltering in the Featherna
     Bush
Look up and say: 'Who owns them hungry hills
That the water-hen and snipe must have forsaken?
A poet? Then by heavens he must be poor'
I hear and is my heart not badly shaken?

CANAL BANK WALK

Leafy-with-love banks and the green waters of the
     canal
Pouring redemption for me, that I do
The will of God, wallow in the habitual, the banal,
Grow with nature again as before I grew.
The bright stick trapped, the breeze adding a third
Party to the couple kissing on an old seat,

PATRICK KAVANAGH

And a bird gathering materials for the nest for the Word
Eloquently new and abandoned to its delirious beat.
O unworn world enrapture me, encapture me in a web
Of fabulous grass and eternal voices by a beech,
Feed the gaping need of my senses, give me ad lib
To pray unselfconsciously with overflowing speech
For this soul needs to be honoured with a new dress woven
From green and blue things and arguments that cannot be proven.

IS

The important thing is not
To imagine one ought
Have something to say,
A raison d'etre, a plot for the play.
The only true teaching
Subsists in watching
Things moving or just colour
Without comment from the scholar.
To look on is enough
In the business of love.
Casually remark
On a deer running in a park;
Mention water again
Always virginal,
Always original,
It washes out Original Sin.
Name for the future
The everydays of nature
And without being analytic
Create a great epic.
Girls in red blouses,

Steps up to houses,
Sunlight round gables,
Gossip's young fables,
The life of a street.

O wealthy me! O happy state!
With an inexhaustible theme
I'll die in harness,
I'll die in harness with my scheme.

PATRICK KAVANAGH

TO HELL WITH COMMONSENSE

More kicks than pence
We get from commonsense
Above its door is writ
All hope abandon. It
Is a bank will refuse a post
Dated cheque of the Holy Ghost.
Therefore I say to hell
With all reasonable
Poems in particular
We want no secular
Wisdom plodded together
By concerned fools. Gather
No moss you rolling stones
Nothing thought out atones
For no flight
In the light.
Let them wear out nerve and bone
Those who would have it that way
But in the end nothing that they
Have achieved will be in the shake up

PATRICK KAVAN-AGH

In the final Wake Up
And I have a feeling
That through the hole in reason's ceiling
We can fly to knowledge
Without ever going to college.

DEAR FOLKS

Just a line to remind my friends that after much trouble
Of one kind and another I am back in circulation.
I have recovered most of my heirlooms from the humps of rubble
That once was the house where I lived in the name of a nation.
And precious little I assure you was worth mind storage:
The images of half a dozen women who fell for the unusual,
For the Is that Is and the laughter-smothered courage,
The poet's. And I also found some crucial
Documents of sad evil that may yet
For all their ugliness and vacuous leers
Fuel the fires of comedy. The main thing is to continue,
To walk Parnassus right into the sunset
Detached in love where pygmies cannot pin you
To the ground like Gulliver. So good luck and cheers.

LECTURE HALL

To speak in summer in a lecture hall
About literature and its use
I pick my brains and tease out all
To see if I can choose
Something untarnished, some new news

From experience that has been immediate,   PATRICK
Recent, something that makes   KAVAN-
The listener or reader   AGH
Impregnant, something that reinstates
The poet. A few words like birth-dates

That brings him back in the public mind,
I mean the mind of the dozen or so
Who constantly listen out for the two-lined
Message that announces the gusto
Of the dead arisen into the sun-glow.

Someone in America will note
The apparent miracle. In a bar
In Greenwich Village some youthful poet
Will mention it, and a similar
In London or wherever they are

Those pickers-up of messages that produce
The idea that underneath the sun
Things can be new as July dews—
Out of the frowsy, the second-hand won . . .
Keep at it, keep at it while the heat is on

I say to myself as I consider
Virginal crevices in my brain
Where the never-exposed will soon be a mother.
I search for that which has no stain,
Something discovered vividly and sudden.

HOLSTENWALL

We're going to the fair at Holstenwall;
It is my eyes you've taken out—
My bright eyes and my hollow heart
Stare and ring at Holstenwall.

I stand up straight, strong master, stand
Straight as a man, and am no man:
My pulses beat, O master, yet
I can help nothing. This is a wicked land.

Standing and stiff, send me forth, send
My fear forth, master. Cold boards hamper
My fingers, masters, that would grope and clamber
Precise as spiders, grope and rend.

Swift and desiring, master, as a hound,
Let me get life, strong master, tear and wound
These dead crowds into life. O set
My course at this loud land, speed my swift feet.

Set me against the lover and the pope—
I need the living heart, the holy knowledge.
Give me the frightened girl and I will rape
Her life alive and cross the guarded bridge.

We're going to the fair at Holstenwall.
Remember your puppet; life lies in my hand:
Yet no dead doll or clockwork nightingale.
Have pity, master. This is a wicked land.

THE GRAIL

SIDNEY KEYES

The great cup tumbled, ringing like a bell
Thrown down upon the lion-guarded stair
When the cloud took Him; and its iron voice
Challenged the King's dead majesty to fear.

Rise up, Arthur. Galahad grail-seeker
Wails with the pale identical queens on the river.
The sculptured lion raises a clumsy paw:
Bors has lain down beneath the stones of law.

Lie uneasy, Guenever. Lancelot sword-lover
Burnt like a blade will share your bed no more.
Bared his red head, he weeps with shame and
    sickness—
His pride the sword-bridge to your heart of Gorre.

But the dead girl, the flower-crowned, alone
Walks without fear the bannered streets of heaven;
Lies nightly in the hollow of His hand—
The cradle of your fear her fort and haven.

She alone
Knew from her birth the mystic Avalon.

FORD O' KABUL RIVER

Kabul town's by Kabul river—
  Blow the trumpet, draw the sword—
There I lef' my mate for ever,
  Wet an' drippin' by the ford.
    Ford, ford, ford o' Kabul river,
      Ford o' Kabul river in the dark!
    There's the river up an' brimmin', an' there's
      'arf a squadron swimmin'
        'Cross the ford o' Kabul river in the dark.

Kabul town's a blasted place—
  Blow the trumpet, draw the sword—
'Strewth, I shan't forget 'is face
  Wet an' drippin' by the ford!
    Ford, ford, ford o' Kabul river,
      Ford o' Kabul river in the dark!
    Keep the crossing-stakes beside you, an' they
      will surely guide you
        'Cross the ford o' Kabul river in the dark.

Kabul town is sun an' dust—
  Blow the trumpet, draw the sword—
I'd ha' sooner drownded fust
  'Stead of 'im beside the ford.
    Ford, ford, ford o' Kabul river,
      Ford o' Kabul river in the dark!
    You can 'ear the 'orses threshin'; you can 'ear
      the men a-splashin',
        'Cross the ford o' Kabul river in the dark.

Kabul town was ours to take—
  Blow the trumpet, draw the sword—
I'd ha' left it for 'is sake—
  'Im that left me by the ford.
      Ford, ford, ford o' Kabul river,
        Ford o' Kabul river in the dark!
      It's none so bloomin' dry there; ain't you
        never comin' nigh there,
        'Cross the ford o' Kabul river in the dark?

RUDYARD KIPLING

Kabul town'll go to hell—
  Blow the trumpet, draw the sword—
'Fore I see him 'live an' well—
  'Im the best beside the ford.
      Ford, ford, ford o' Kabul river,
        Ford o' Kabul river in the dark!
      Gawd 'elp 'em if they blunder, for their
        boots'll pull 'em under,
        By the ford o' Kabul river in the dark.

Turn your 'orse from Kabul town—
  Blow the bugle, draw the sword—
'Im an' 'arf my troop is down,
  Down and drownded by the ford.
      Ford, ford, ford o' Kabul river,
        Ford o' Kabul river in the dark!
      There's the river low an' fallin', but it ain't
        no use a-callin'
        'Cross the ford o' Kabul river in the dark!

Rudyard Kipling — THE LOOKING GLASS

*Queen Bess was Harry's daughter. Stand forward
    partners all!
In ruff and stomacher and gown
She danced King Philip down-a-down,
And left her shoe to show 'twas true—
(The very tune I'm playing you)
In Norgem at Brickwall!*

The Queen was in her chamber, and she was middling
    old.
Her petticoat was satin, and her stomacher was gold.
Backwards and forwards and sideways did she pass,
Making up her mind to face the cruel looking-glass.
The cruel looking-glass that will never show a lass
As comely or as kindly or as young as what she was!

*Queen Bess was Harry's daughter. Now hand your
    partners all!*

The Queen was in her chamber, a-combing of her
    hair.
There came Queen Mary's spirit and It stood behind
    her chair,
Singing 'Backwards and forwards and sideways may
    you pass,
But I will stand behind you till you face the
    looking-glass.
The cruel looking-glass that will never show a lass
As lovely or unlucky or as lonely as I was!'

*Queen Bess was Harry's daughter. Now turn your
    partners all!*

The Queen was in her chamber, a-weeping very sore,   RUDYARD
There came Lord Leicester's spirit and It scratched   KIPLING
    upon the door,
Singing 'Backwards and forwards and sideways may
    you pass,
But I will walk beside you till you face the
    looking-glass.
The cruel looking-glass that will never show a lass
As hard and unforgiving or as wicked as you was!'

*Queen Bess was Harry's daughter. Now kiss your
    partners all!*

The Queen was in her chamber, her sins were on her
    head,
She looked the spirits up and down and statelily she
    said:-
'Backwards and forwards and sideways though I've
    been,
Yet I am Harry's daughter and I am England's
    Queen!'
And she faced her looking-glass (and whatever else
    there was)
And she saw her day was over and she saw her beauty
    pass
In the cruel looking-glass, that can always hurt a lass
More hard than any ghost there is or any man there
    was!

Rudyard Kipling

GETHSEMANE
1914–18

The Garden called Gethsemane
In Picardy it was,
And there the people came to see
The English soldiers pass.
We used to pass—we used to pass
Or halt, as it might be,
And ship our masks in case of gas
Beyond Gethsemane.

The Garden called Gethsemane,
It held a pretty lass,
But all the time she talked to me
I prayed my cup might pass.
The officer sat on the chair,
The men lay on the grass,
And all the time we halted there
I prayed my cup might pass.

It didn't pass—it didn't pass—
It didn't pass from me.
I drank it when we met the gas
Beyond Gethsemane.

FIVE WAR EPITAPHS

I. COMMON FORM

If any question why we died,
Tell them, because our fathers lied.

II. THE BEGINNER

On the first hour of my first day
In the front trench I fell.
(Children in boxes at a play
Stand up to watch it well.)

III. THE REFINED MAN

I was of delicate mind. I stepped aside for my needs,
Disdaining the common office. I was seen from afar
    and killed ...
How is this matter for mirth? Let each man be judged
    by his deeds.
*I have paid my price to live with myself on the terms that
    I willed.*

IV. 'EQUALITY OF SACRIFICE'

A. 'I was a Have.'   B. 'I was a "Have-not." '
(*Together*) 'What hast thou given which I gave not?'

V. THE COWARD

I could not look on Death, which being known,
Men led me to him, blindfold and alone.

A CORRECT COMPASSION

To Mr. Philip Allison, after watching him perform a Mitral Stenosis Valvulotomy in the General Infirmary at Leeds.

Cleanly, sir, you went to the core of the matter.
Using the purest kind of wit, a balance of belief and art,
You with a curious nervous elegance laid bare
The root of life, and put your finger on its beating heart.

The glistening theatre swarms with eyes, and hands, and eyes.
On green-clothed tables, ranks of instruments transmit a sterile gleam.
The masks are on, and no unnecessary smile betrays
A certain tension, true concomitant of calm.

Here we communicate by looks, though words,
Too, are used, as in continuous historic present
You describe our observations and your deeds.
All gesture is reduced to its result, an instrument.

She who does not know she is a patient lies
Within a tent of green, and sleeps without a sound
Beneath the lamps, and the reflectors that devise
Illuminations probing the profoundest wound.

A calligraphic master, improvising, you invent
The first incision, and no poet's hesitation

Before his snow-blank page mars your intent:
The flowing stroke is drawn like an uncalculated
    inspiration.

A garland of flowers unfurls across the painted
    flesh.
With quick precision the arterial forceps click.
Yellow threads are knotted with a simple flourish.
Transfused, the blood preserves its rose, though it is
    sick.

Meters record the blood, measure heart-beats,
    control the breath.
Hieratic gesture: scalpel bares a creamy rib; with
    pincer knives
The bone quietly is clipped, and lifted out. Beneath,
The pink, black-mottled lung like a revolted creature
    heaves,

Collapses; as if by extra fingers is neatly held aside
By two ordinary egg-beaters, kitchen tools that
    curve
Like extraordinary hands. Heart, laid bare, silently
    beats. It can hide
No longer, yet is not revealed.—'A local anaesthetic
    in the cardiac nerve.'

Now, in firm hands that quiver with a careful
    strength,
Your knife feels through the heart's transparent skin;
    at first,
Inside the pericardium, slit down half its length,
The heart, black-veined, swells like a fruit about to
    burst,

JAMES KIRKUP But goes on beating, love's poignant image bleeding at the dart
Of a more grievous passion, as a bird, dreaming of flight, sleeps on
Within its leafy cage.—'It generally upsets the heart
A bit, though not unduly, when I make the first injection.'

Still, still the patient sleeps, and still the speaking heart is dumb.
The watchers breathe an air far sweeter, rarer than the room's.
The cold walls listen. Each in his own blood hears the drum
She hears, tented in green, unfathomable calms.

'I make a purse-string suture here, with a reserve
Suture, which I must make first, and deeper,
As a safeguard, should the other burst. In the cardiac nerve
I inject again a local anaesthetic. Could we have fresh towels to cover

All these adventitious ones. Now can you all see?
When I put my finger inside the valve, there may be a lot
Of blood, and it may come with quite a bang. But I let it flow,
In case there are any clots, to give the heart a good clean-out.

Now can you give me every bit of light you've got'.
We stand on the benches, peering over his shoulder.

The lamp's intensest rays are concentrated on an JAMES
    inmost heart. KIRKUP
Someone coughs.—'If you have to cough, you will do
    it outside this theatre.'
                    '—Yes, sir.'

'How's she breathing, Doug.? Do you feel quite
    happy?'—
                —'Yes fairly
Happy'.—'Now. I am putting my finger in the
    opening of the valve.
I can only get the tip of my finger in.—It's gradually
Giving way.—I'm inside.—No clots.—I can feel the
    valve

Breathing freely now around my finger, and the heart
    working.
Not too much blood. It opened very nicely.
I should say that anatomically speaking
This is a perfect case.—Anatomically.

For of course, anatomy is not physiology'.
We find we breathe again, and hear the surgeon hum.
Outside, in the street, a car starts up. The heart
    regularly
Thunders.—'I do not stitch up the pericardium.

It is not necessary.' For this is imagination's other
    place,
Where only necessary things are done, with the
    supreme and grave
Dexterity that ignores technique; with proper grace
Informing a correct compassion, that performs its
    love, and makes it live.

PHILIP LARKIN

AMBULANCES

Closed like confessionals, they thread
Loud noons of cities, giving back
None of the glances they absorb.
Light glossy grey, arms on a plaque,
They come to rest at any kerb:
All streets in time are visited.

Then children strewn on steps or road,
Or women coming from the shops
Past smells of different dinners, see
A wild white face that overtops
Red stretcher-blankets momently
As it is carried in and stowed,

And sense the solving emptiness
That lies just under all we do,
And for a second get it whole,
So permanent and blank and true.
The fastened doors recede. *Poor soul*,
They whisper at their own distress;

For borne away in deadened air
May go the sudden shut of loss
Round something nearly at an end,
And what cohered in it across
The years, the unique random blend
Of families and fashions, there

At last begin to loosen. Far
From the exchange of love to lie
Unreachable inside a room
The traffic parts to let go by
Brings closer what is left to come,
And dulls to distance all we are.

D. H. LAWRENCE

THE SHIP OF DEATH

I

Now it is autumn and the falling fruit
and the long journey towards oblivion.

The apples falling like great drops of dew
to bruise themselves an exit from themselves.

And it is time to go, to bid farewell
to one's own self, and find an exit
from the fallen self.

II

Have you built your ship of death, O have you?
O build your ship of death, for you will need it.

The grim frost is at hand, when the apples will fall
thick, almost thundrous, on the hardened earth.

And death is on the air like a smell of ashes!
Ah! can't you smell it?
And in the bruised body, the frightened soul
finds itself shrinking, wincing from the cold
that blows upon it through the orifices.

III

And can a man his own quietus make
with a bare bodkin?

D. H. LAW-
RENCE

    With daggers, bodkins, bullets, man can make
a bruise or break of exit for his life;
but is that a quietus, O tell me, is it quietus?

>   Surely not so! for how could murder, even self-
>   murder
>   ever a quietus make?

IV

> O let us talk of quiet that we know,
> that we can know, the deep and lovely quiet
> of a strong heart at peace!
>
> How can we this, our own quietus, make?

V

> Build then the ship of death, for you must take
> the longest journey, to oblivion.
>
> And die the death, the long and painful death
> that lies between the old self and the new.
>
> Already our bodies are fallen, bruised, badly bruised,
> already our souls are oozing through the exit
> of the cruel bruise.
>
> Already the dark endless ocean of the end
> is washing in through the breaches of our wounds,
> already the flood is upon us.
>
> O build your ship of death, your little ark
> and furnish it with food, with little cakes, and wine
> for the dark flight down oblivion.

VI

Piecemeal the body dies, and the timid soul
has her footing washed away, as the dark flood rises.

We are dying, we are dying, we are all of us dying
and nothing will stay the death-flood rising within us
and soon it will rise on the world, on the outside
    world.

We are dying, we are dying, piecemeal our bodies are
    dying
and our strength leaves us,
and our soul cowers naked in the dark rain over the
    flood,
cowering in the last branches of the tree of our life.

VII

We are dying, we are dying, so all we can do
is now to be willing to die, and to build the ship
of death to carry the soul on the longest journey.

A little ship, with oars and food
and little dishes, and all accoutrements
fitting and ready for the departing soul.

Now launch the small ship, now as the body dies
and life departs, launch out, the fragile soul
in the fragile ship of courage, the ark of faith
with its store of food and little cooking pans
and change of clothes,
upon the flood's black waste
upon the waters of the end
upon the sea of death, where still we sail
darkly, for we cannot steer, and have no port.

D. H. Lawrence

There is no port, there is nowhere to go
only the deepening blackness darkening still
blacker upon the soundless, ungurgling flood
darkness at one with darkness, up and down
and sideways utterly dark, so there is no direction
    any more
and the little ship is there; yet she is gone.
She is not seen, for there is nothing to see her by.
She is gone! gone! and yet
somewhere she is there.
Nowhere!

VIII

And everything is gone, the body is gone
completely under, gone, entirely gone.
The upper darkness is heavy as the lower,
between them the little ship
is gone.
It is the end, it is oblivion.

And yet out of eternity, a thread
separates itself on the blackness,
a horizontal thread
that fumes a little with pallor upon the dark.

Is it illusion? or does the pallor fume
a little higher?
Ah wait, wait, for there's the dawn,
the cruel dawn of coming back to life
out of oblivion.

Wait, wait, the little ship   D. H.
drifting, beneath the deathly ashy grey   LAW-
of a flood-dawn.   RENCE

Wait, wait! even so, a flush of yellow
and strangely, O chilled wan soul, a flush or rose.

A flush or rose, and the whole thing starts again.

x

The flood subsides, and the body, like a worn sea-shell
emerges strange and lovely.
And the little ship wings home, faltering and lapsing
    on the pink flood,
and the frail soul steps out, into the house again
filling the heart with peace.

Swings the heart renewed with peace
even of oblivion.

O build your ship of death. O build it!
for you will need it.
For the voyage of oblivion awaits you.

MILKMAID

The girl's far treble, muted to the heat,
calls like a fainting bird across the fields
to where her flock lies panting for her voice,
their black horns buried deep in marigolds.

They climb awake, like drowsy butterflies,
and press their red flanks through the tall branched
    grass,
and as they go their wandering tongues embrace
the vacant summer mirrored in their eyes.

Led to the limestone shadows of a barn
they snuff their past embalmed in the hay,
while her cool hand, cupped to the udder's fount,
distils the brimming harvest of their day.

Look what a cloudy cream the earth gives out,
fat juice of buttercups and meadow-rye;
the girl dreams milk within her body's field
and hears, far off, her muted children cry.

ALUN LEWIS

TO A COMRADE IN ARMS

Red fool, my laughing comrade,
Hiding your woman's love
And your man's madness,
Patrolling farther than nowhere
To gain what is nearer than here,
Your face will grow grey as Christ's garments
With the dust of ditches and trenches,
So endlessly faring.

Red fool, my laughing comrade,
Hiding your mystic symbols
Of bread broken for eating
And palm-leaves strewn for welcome,
What foe will you make your peace with
This summer that is more cruel
Than the ancient God of the Hebrews?

When bees swarm in your nostrils
And honey drips from the sockets
Of eyes that today are frantic
With love that is frustrate,
What vow shall we vow who love you
For the self that you did not value?

C. DAY LEWIS

NEARING AGAIN THE LEGENDARY ISLE

(*From* The Magnetic Mountain)

Nearing again the legendary isle
Where sirens sang and mariners were skinned,
We wonder now what was there to beguile
That such stout fellows left their bones behind.

Those chorus-girls are surely past their prime,
Voices grow shrill and paint is wearing thin,
Lips that sealed up the sense from gnawing time
Now beg the favour with a graveyard grin.

We have no flesh to spare and they can't bite,
Hunger and sweat have stripped us to the bone;
A skeleton crew we toil upon the tide
And mock the theme-song meant to lure us on:

No need to stop the ears, avert the eyes
From purple rhetoric of evening skies.

NOW SHE IS LIKE THE WHITE TREE-ROSE   C. Day Lewis

(*From* From Feathers to Iron)

Now she is like the white tree-rose
That takes a blessing from the sun:
Summer has filled her veins with light,
And her warm heart is washed with noon.

Or as a poplar, ceaselessly
Gives a soft answer to the wind:
Cool on the light her leaves lie sleeping,
Folding a column of sweet sound.

Powder the stars. Forbid the night
To wear those brilliants for a brooch
So soon, dark death, you may close down
The mines that made this beauty rich.

Her thoughts are pleiads, stooping low
O'er glades where nightingale has flown:
And like the luminous night around her
She has at heart a certain dawn.

THE SONG OF
THE MILITANT ROMANCE

i

Again let me do a lot of extraordinary talking.
Again let me do a lot!
Let me abound in speeches—let me abound!—publicly polyglot.
Better a blind word to bluster with—better a bad word than none lieber Gott!
Watch me push into my witch's vortex all the Englishman's got
To cackle and rattle with—you catch my intention?—to be busily balking
The tongue-tied Briton—that is my outlandish plot!

To put a spark in his damp peat—a squib for the Scotchman—
Starch for the Irish—to give a teutonic-cum-Scot
Breadth to all that is slender in Anglo-cum-Oxfordshire-Saxony,
Over-pretty in Eire—to give to this watery galaxy
A Norseman's seasalted stamina, a dram of the Volsung's salt blood.

ii

As to the trick of the prosody, the method of conveying the matter,
Frankly I shall provoke the maximum of saxophone clatter.
I shall not take 'limping' iambics, nor borrow from Archilochous

His 'light-horse gallop', nor drive us into a short WYND-
   distich that would bog us. HAM
I shall *not* go back to Sheltonics, nor listen to Doctor LEWIS
   Guest.
I know with my bold Fourteener I have the measure
   that suits us best.
I shall drive the matter along as I have driven it from
   the first,
My peristalsis is well-nigh perfect in burst upon
   well-timed burst—
I shall drive my coach and four through the strictest
   of hippical treatises,
I do not want to know too closely the number of
   beats it is.
So shipwreck the nerves to enable the vessel the
   better to float.
This cockle shell's what it first was built for, and a
   most seaworthy boat.
At roll-call *Byron Dominus* uttered at a fool-school,
Shouted by scottish ushers, caused his lordship to sob
   like a fool,
Yet Byron was the first to laugh at the over-sensitive
   Keats
'Snuffed out by an article', those were the words. A
   couple of rubber teats
Should have been supplied beyond any question to
   these over-touchy pets—
For me, you are free to spit your hardest and explode
   your bloody spleen
Regarding my bold compact Fourteener, or my four
   less than fourteen.

iii

So set up a shouting for me! Get a Donnybrook
   racket on!

WYNDHAM LEWIS
Hound down the drowsy latin goliaths that clutter the lexicon—
Send a contingent over to intone in our battle-line—
Wrench the trumpet out of the centre of a monkish leonine—
Courtmartial the stripling slackers who dance in the dull Rhyme Royal—
Send staggering out all the stammerers who stick round as Chaucer's foil—
Dig out the dogs from the doggerel of the hudibrastic couplet—
Hot up the cold-as-mutton songbirds of the plantagenet cabinet!
Go back to the Confessor's palace and disentangle some anglo-saxon,
And borrow a bellow or two from the pictish or from the Manxman.
Set all our mother-tongue reeling, with the eruption of obsolete vocables,
Disrupt it with all the grammars, that are ground down to cement it—with obstacles
Strew all the cricket pitches, the sleek tennis-lawns of our tongue—
Instal a nasty cold in our larynx—a breathlessness in our lung!

iv

But let me have silence always, in the centre of the shouting—
That is essential! Let me have silence so that no pin may drop
And not be heard, and not a whisper escape us for all our spouting,
Nor the needle's scratching upon this gramophone of a circular cosmic spot.

Hear me! Mark me! Learn me! Throw the mind's ear WYND-
    open—   HAM
Shut up the mind's eye—all will be music! What   LEWIS
Sculpture of sound cannot—what cannot as a fluid token
Words—that nothing else cannot!

v

But when the great blind talking is set up and
    thoroughly got going—
When you are accustomed to be stunned—
When the thunder of this palaver breaks with a
    gentle soughing
Of discreet Zephyrs, or of dull surf underground—
Full-roaring, when sinus sinus is outblowing,
Backed up by a bellow of sheer blarney loudest-
    lunged—
That is the moment to compel from speech
That hybrid beyond language—hybrid only words
    can reach.

vi

Break out word-storms!—a proper tongue-burst!
    Split
Our palate down the middle—shatter it!
Give us hare-lip and cross us with a seal
That we may emit the most ear-splitting squeal!
Let words forsake their syntax and ambit—
The dam of all the lexicons gone west!—
Chaos restored, why then by such storms hit
The brain can mint its imagery best.
Whoever heard of perfect sense or perfect rhythm
Matching the magic of extreme verbal schism?

vii

Swept off your feet, be on the look out for the pattern.
It is the chart that matters—the graph is everything!

WYND-　In such wild weather you cannot look too closely at
HAM　　 'em—
LEWIS Cleave to the abstract of this blossoming.
　　　　I shall, I perhaps should say, make use of a duplicate screen—
　　　　An upper and a lower (the pattern lies between)
　　　　But most observe the understrapper—the second-string.
　　　　The counterpart's the important—keep your eye on the copy—
　　　　What's plainest seen is a mere buffer. But if that's too shoppy,
　　　　Just say to yourself—'He talks around the compass
　　　　To get back at last to the thing that started all the rumpus!'

viii

Do not expect a work of the classic canon.
Take binoculars to these nests of camouflage—
Spy out what is *half-there*—the page-under-the-page.
Never demand the integral—never completion—
Always what is fragmentary—the promise, the presage—
Eavesdrop upon the soliloquy—stop calling the spade spade—
Neglecting causes always in favour of their effects—
Reading between the lines—surprising things half-made—
Preferring shapes spurned by our intellects.
Plump for the thing, however odd, that's ready to do duty for another,
Sooner than one kowtowing to causation and the living-image of its mother.

ix WYNDHAM LEWIS

Do your damnedest! Be yourself! Be an honest-to-goodness sport!
Take all on trust! Shut up the gift-nag's mouth! Batten upon report!
And you'll hear a great deal more, where a sentence breaks in two,
Believe me, than ever the most certificated schoolmaster's darlings do!
When a clause breaks down (that's natural, for it's been probably overtaxed)
Or the sense is observed to squint, or in a dashing grammatical tort,
You'll find more of the stuff of poetry than ever in stupid syntax!

I sabotage the sentence! With me is the naked word.
I spike the verb—all parts of speech are pushed over on their backs.
I am the master of all that is half-uttered and imperfectly heard.
Return with me where I am crying out with the gorilla and the bird!

DELIRIUM IN VERA CRUZ

Where has tenderness gone, he asked the mirror
Of the Biltmore Hotel, cuarto 216. Alas,
Can its reflection lean against the glass
Too, wondering where I have gone, into what horror?
Is that it staring at me now with terror
Behind your frail tilted barrier? Tenderness
Was here, in this very bedroom, in this
Place, its form seen, cries heard, by you. What error
Is here? Am I that rashed image?
Is this the ghost of the love you reflected?
Now with a background of tequila, stubs, dirty collars,
Sodium perborate, and a scrawled page
To the dead, telephone off the hook? In rage
He smashed all the glass in the room. (Bill: $50.)

AFTER PUBLICATION OF UNDER THE VOLCANO

Success is like some horrible disaster
Worse than your house burning, the sounds of ruination
As the roof tree falls following each other faster
While you stand, the helpless witness of your damnation.

Fame like a drunkard consumes the house of the soul
Exposing that you have worked for only this—
Ah, that I had never suffered this treacherous kiss
And had been left in darkness forever to founder and fail.

HUGH MACDIARMID

THE TWO PARENTS

I love my little son, and yet when he was ill
I could not confine myself to his bedside.
I was impatient of his squalid little needs,
His laboured breathing, and the fretful way he cried,
And longed for my wide range of interests again,
Whereas his mother sank without another care
To that dread level of nothing but life itself
And stayed, day and night, till he was better, there.

Women may pretend, yet they always dismiss
Everything but mere being just like this.

O WHA'S BEEN HERE AFORE ME, LASS

O wha's been here afore me, lass,
And hoo did he get in?
—*A man that deed or I was born*
This evil thing has din.

And left as it were on a corpse
Your maidenheid tae me?
—*Nae lass, gudeman, sin' time began*
'S had ony mair to gi'e.

But I can gi'e ye kindness, lad,
And a pair o' willing hands,
And you sall ha'e my breists like stars,
My limbs like willow wands,

*And on my lips ye'll heed nae mair,
And in my hair forget,
The seed o' a' the men that in
My virgin womb ha'e met.*

SCUNNER

Your body derns
In its graces again
As the dreich grun' does
In the gowden grain,
And out o' the daith
O' pride you rise
Wi' beauty yet
For a hauf-disguise.

The skinklan' stars
Are but distant dirt.
Tho' fer owre near
You are still—whiles—girt
Wi' the bonny licht
You bood hae tint
—And I lo'e Love
Wi' a scunner in't.

EMPTY VESSEL

I met ayont the cairney
A lass wi' tousie hair
Singin' till a bairnie
That was nae langer there.

Wunds wi' warlds to swing
Dinna sing sae sweet.
The licht that bends owre a' thing
Is less ta'en up wi't.

BRITISH LEFTISH POETRY, 1930–40   HUGH MACDIARMID

Auden, MacNeice, Day Lewis, I have read them all,
Hoping against hope to hear the authentic call.
'A tragical disappointment. There was I
Hoping to hear old Aeschylus, when the Herald
Called out, "Theognis, bring your chorus forward."
Imagine what my feelings must have been!
But then Dexitheus pleased me coming forward
And singing his Bœotian melody:
But next came Chaeris with his music truly
That turned me sick and killed me very nearly.
And never in my lifetime, man nor boy,
Was I so vexed as at the present moment;
To see the Pynx, at this time of the morning,
Quite empty, when the Assembly should be full'†
And know the explanation I must pass is this
—You cannot light a match on a crumbling wall.

REFLECTIONS IN A SLUM

A lot of the old folk here—all that's left
Of them after a lifetime's infernal thrall
Remind me of a Bolshie the 'whites' buried alive
Up to his nose, just able to breathe, that's all.
Watch them. You'll see what I mean. When found
His eyes had lost their former gay twinkle.
Ants had eaten *that* away; but there was still
Some life in him ... his forehead *would* wrinkle!
And I remember Gide telling
Of Valéry and himself:
'It was a long time ago. We were young.
We had mingled with idlers
Who formed a circle
Round a troupe of wretched mountebanks.

† Aristophanes' *The Acharnians*

HUGH It was on a raised strip of pavement
MAC- In the boulevard Saint-Germain,
DIARMID In front of the Statue of Broca.
   They were admiring a poor woman,
   Thin and gaunt, in pink tights, despite the cold.
   Her team-mate had tied her, trussed her up,
   Skilfully from head to foot,
   With a rope that went round her
   I don't know how many times,
   And from which, by a sort of wriggling,
   She was to manage to free herself.

   Sorry image of the fate of the masses!
   But no one thought of the symbol.
   The audience merely contemplated
   In stupid bliss the patient's efforts
   She twisted, she writhed, slowly freed one arm,
   Then the other, and when at last
   The final cord fell from her
   Valéry took me by the arm:
   'Let's go now! She has ceased suffering!'

   Oh, if only ceasing to suffer
   They were able to become men.
   Alas! how many owe their dignity,
   Their claim on our sympathy,
   Merely to their misfortune.
   Likewise, so long as a plant has not blossomed
   One can hope that its flowering will be beautiful.
   What a mirage surrounds what has not yet blossomed!
   What a disappointment when one can no longer
   Blame the abjection on the deficiency!
   It is good that the voice of the indigent
   Too long stifled, should manage
   To make itself heard.

But I cannot consent to listen
To nothing but that voice.
Man does not cease to interest me
When he ceases to be miserable.
Quite the contrary!
That it is important to aid him
In the beginning goes without saying,
Like a plant it is essential
To water at first,
But this is in order to let it to flower
And I *am concerned with the blossom.*

HUGH
MAC-
DIARMID

SHE WALKED UNAWARE

O, she walked unaware of her own increasing beauty
That was holding men's thoughts from market or
    plough,
As she passed by intent on her womanly duties
And she without leisure to be wayward or proud;
Or if she had pride then it was not in her thinking
But thoughtless in her body like a flower of good
    breeding.
The first time I saw her spreading coloured linen
Beyond the green willow she gave me gentle greeting
With no more intention than the leaning willow tree.

Though she smiled without intention yet from that
    day forward
Her beauty filled like water the four corners of my
    being,
And she rested in my heart like a hare in the form
That is shaped to herself. And I that would be singing
Or whistling at all times went silently then;
Till I drew her aside among straight stems of beeches
When the blackbird was sleeping, and she promised
    that never
The fields would be ripe but I'd gather all sweetness,
A red moon of August would rise on our wedding.

October is spreading bright flame along stripped
    willows,
Low fires of the dogwood burn down to grey water,—
God pity me now and all desolate sinners

Demented with beauty! I have blackened my thought   PATRICK
In drouths of bad longing, and all brightness goes   MAC-
    shrouded   DONOGH
Since he came with his rapture of wild words that
    mirrored
Her beauty and made her ungentle and proud.
To-night she will spread her brown hair on his pillow,
But I shall be hearing the harsh cries of wild fowl.

LOUIS MACNEICE

THE MIXER

With a pert moustache and a ready candid smile
He has played his way through twenty years of pubs,
Deckchairs, lounges, touchlines, junctions, homes,
And still as ever popular, he roams
Far and narrow, mimicking the style
Of other people's leisure, scattering stubs.

Colourless, when alone, and self-accused,
He is only happy in reflected light
And only real in the range of laughter;
Behind his eyes are shadows of a night
In Flanders but his mind long since refused
To let that time intrude on what came after.

So in this second war which is fearful too,
He cannot away with silence but has grown
Almost a cypher, like a Latin word
That many languages have made their own
Till it is worn and blunt and easy to construe
And often spoken but no longer heard.

CHARON

The conductor's hands were black with money:
Hold on to your ticket, he said, the inspector's
Mind is black with suspicion, and hold on to
That dissolving map. We moved through London,
We could see the pigeons through the glass but failed
To hear their rumours of wars, we could see

LOUIS MAC-NEICE

The lost dog barking but never knew
That his bark was as shrill as a cock crowing,
We just jogged on, at each request
Stop there was a crowd of aggressively vacant
Faces, we just jogged on, eternity
Gave itself airs in revolving lights
And then we came to the Thames and all
The bridges were down, the further shore
Was lost in fog, so we asked the conductor
What we should do. He said: Take the ferry
Faute de mieux. We flicked the flashlight
And there was the ferryman just as Virgil
And Dante had seen him. He looked at us coldly
And his eyes were dead and his hands on the oar
Were black with obols and varicose veins
Marbled his hands and he said to us coldly:
If you want to die you will have to pay for it.

SEA-CHANGE

'Goneys an' gullies an' all o' the birds o' the sea
They ain't no birds, not really,' said Billy the Dane.
'Not mollies, nor gullies, nor goneys at all,' said he,
'But simply the sperrits of mariners livin' again.

'Them birds goin' fishin' is nothin' but souls o' the
    drowned,
Souls o' the drowned an' the kicked as are never no
    more;
An' that there haughty old albatross cruisin' around,
Belike he's Admiral Nelson or Admiral Noah.

'An' merry's the life they are living. They settle and
    dip,
They fishes, they never stands watches, they waggle
    their wings;
When a ship comes by, they fly to look at the ship
To see how the nowaday mariners manages things.

'When freezing aloft in a snorter, I tell you I wish—
(Though maybe it ain't like a Christian)—I wish I
    could be
A haughty old copper-bound albatross dipping for fish
And coming the proud over all o' the birds o' the sea.'

HAROLD MONRO

THE TERRIBLE DOOR

Too long outside your door I have shivered.
You open it? I will not stay.
I'm haunted by your ashen beauty.
Take back your hand. I have gone away.

Don't talk, but move to that near corner.
I loathe the long cold shadow here.
We will stand a moment in the lamplight,
Until I watch you hard and near.

Happy release! Good-bye for ever!
Here at the corner we say good-bye.
But if you want me, if you need me
Who waits, at the terrible door, but I?

STREET FIGHT

From prehistoric distance, beyond clocks,
Fear radiates to life
And thrills onto the elbows of two men.
Fear drives imagination to renew
Their prehistoric interrupted throttle.

The street turns out and runs about,
And windows rise, and women scream;
Their husbands grunt, or scratch and hunt
Their heads, but cannot trace the dream.

Meanwhile those:
They rush; they close:

HAROLD flick, flap, bang, bang, blood, sweat, stars, moon,
MONRO push, roar, rush, hold, part, bang, grind, swoon,
        O slow, O swift, O now—But soon,

How soon the heavy policeman rolls in sight,
And barges slowly through that little crowd,
And lays his large hands calmly on those shoulders.
Now all will be exactly as it should be,
And everybody quietly go to bed.

Occasional spectator,
Do not you think it was very entertaining?
You, standing behind your vast round belly,
With your truss, your operation scar,

Your hairless head, your horn-rimmed eyes,
Your varicose veins,
Neuritis, neurasthenia, rheumatism,
Flat-foot walking, awkward straining of sinews,
Over the whole of your body
The slowly advancing pains approaching death,
What comes into your mind when two men fight?

T. STURGE MOORE

A DAUGHTER OF ADMETUS

Apollo kept my father's sheep,
For love of him I cannot sleep;
Far on the hills a dog will bark;
The stars move browsing up the dark;
Their lambs, like dust for number, graze
On night and fill me with amaze;
Brooding how he now tells the tale
Of yonder flock, has worn me pale;
My fingers ache to comb his locks;
All wings for wonder my heart knocks
Against her cage . . . would dash abroad,
Head for, and nest with her adored!

RICHARD MURPHY

EPITAPH ON A FIR-TREE

She grew ninety years through sombre winter,
Rhododendron summer of midges and rain,
In a beechwood scarred by the auctioneer,

Till a March evening, the garden work done,
It seemed her long life had been completed,
No further growth, no gaiety could remain.

At a wedding breakfast bridesmaids planted
With trowel and gloves this imported fir.
How soon, measured by trees, the party ended.

Arbour and crinoline have gone under
The laurel, gazebos under the yews:
Wood for wood, we have little to compare.

We think no more of granite steps and pews,
Or an officer patched with a crude trepan
Who fought in Rangoon for these quiet acres.

Axes and saws now convert the evergreen
Imperial shadows into deal boards,
And let the sun enter our house again.

Quickly we'll spend the rings that she hoarded
In her gross girth. The evening is ours.
Those delicate girls who earthed her up are faded.

Except for daffodils, the ground is bare:
We two are left. They walked through pergolas
And planted well, so that we might do better.

EDWIN MUIR

THE WAYSIDE STATION

Here at the wayside station, as many a morning,
I watch the smoke torn from the fumy engine
Crawling across the fields in serpent sorrow.
Flat in the east, held down by stolid clouds,
The struggling day is born and shines already
On its warm hearth far off. Yet something here
Glimmers along the ground to show the seagulls
White on the furrows' black unturning waves.

But now the light has broadened.
I watch the farmstead on the little hill,
That seems to mutter: 'Here is day again'
Unwillingly. Now the sad cattle wake
In every byre and stall,
The ploughboy stirs in the loft, the farmer groans
And feels the day like a familiar ache
Deep in his body, though the house is dark.
The lovers part
Now in the bedroom where the pillows gleam
Great and mysterious as deep hills of snow,
An inaccessible land. The wood stands waiting
While the bright snare slips coil by coil around it,
Dark silver on every branch. The lonely stream
That rode through darkness leaps the gap of light,
Its voice grown loud, and starts its winding journey
Through the day and time and war and history.

EDWIN MUIR

THE CHILD DYING

Unfriendly friendly universe,
I pack your stars into my purse,
And bid you, bid you so farewell.
That I can leave you, quite go out,
Go out, go out beyond all doubt,
My father says, is the miracle.

You are so great, and I so small:
I am nothing, you are all:
Being nothing, I can take this way.
Oh I need neither rise nor fall,
For when I do not move at all
I shall be out of all your day.

It's said some memory will remain
In the other place, grass in the rain,
Light on the land, sun on the sea,
A flitting grace, a phantom face,
But the world is out. There is no place
Where it and its ghost can ever be.

Father, father, I dread this air
Blown from the far side of despair,
The cold cold corner. What house, what hold,
What hand is there? I look and see
Nothing-filled eternity,
And the great round world grows weak and old.

Hold my hand, oh hold it fast—
I am changing!—until at last
My hand in yours no more will change,
Though yours change on. You here, I there,
So hand in hand, twin-leafed despair—
I did not know death was so strange.

MERLIN

EDWIN MUIR

O Merlin in your crystal cave
Deep in the diamond of the day,
Will there ever be a singer
Whose music will smooth away
The furrow drawn by Adam's finger
Across the meadow and the wave?
Or a runner who'll outrun
Man's long shadow driving on,
Break through the gate of memory
And hang the apple on the tree?
Will your magic ever show
The sleeping bride shut in her bower,
The day wreathed in its mound of snow
And Time locked in his tower?

SONG

(*To an air by Henry Lawes, published in* 1652)

The flowers that in thy garden rise,
Fade and are gone when Summer flies,
And as their sweets by time decay,
So shall thy hopes be cast away.

The Sun that gilds the creeping moss
Stayeth not Earth's eternal loss:
He is the lord of all that live,
Yet there is life he cannot give.

The stir of Morning's eager breath—
Beautiful Eve's impassioned death—
Thou lovest these, thou lovest well,
Yet of the Night thou canst not tell.

In every land thy feet may tread,
Time like a veil is round thy head:
Only the land thou seek'st with me
Never hath been nor yet shall be.

It is not far, it is not near,
Name it hath none that Earth can hear;
But there thy Soul shall build again
Memories long destroyed of men,
And Joy thereby shall like a river
Wander from deep to deep for ever.

FROM GENERATION TO GENERATION

HENRY NEWBOLT

O Son of mine, when dusk shall find thee bending
Between a gravestone and a cradle's head—
Between the love whose name is loss unending
And the young love whose thoughts are liker dread,—
Thou too shalt groan at heart that all thy spending
Cannot repay the dead, the hungry dead.

COMMEMORATION

I sat by the granite pillar, and sunlight fell
Where the sunlight fell of old,
And the hour was the hour my heart remembered well,
And the sermon rolled and rolled
As it used to roll when the place was still unhaunted,
And the strangest tale in the world was still untold.

And I knew that of all this rushing of urgent sound
That I so clearly heard,
The green young forest of saplings clustered round
Was heeding not one word:
Their heads were bowed in a still serried patience
Such as an angel's breath could never have stirred.

For some were already away to the hazardous pitch,
Or lining the parapet wall,
And some were in glorious battle, or great and rich,
Or throned in a college hall:
And among the rest was one like my own young phantom,
Dreaming for ever beyond my utmost call.

HENRY NEWBOLT 'O Youth,' the preacher was crying, 'deem not thou
Thy life is thine alone;
    Thou bearest the will of the ages, seeing how
    They built thee bone by bone,
    And within thy blood the Great Age sleeps sepulchred
Till thou and thine shall roll away the stone.

'Therefore the days are coming when thou shalt burn
    With passion whitely hot;
Rest shall be rest no more; thy feet shall spurn
    All that thy hand hath got;
And One that is stronger shall gird thee, and lead thee swiftly
    Whither, O heart of Youth, thou wouldest not.'

And the School passed; and I saw the living and the dead
    Set in their seats again,
And I longed to hear them speak of the word that was said,
    But I knew that I longed in vain.
And they stretched forth their hands, and the wind of the spirit took them
Lightly as drifted leaves on an endless plain.

ROBERT NICHOLS

HARLOTS' CATCH

Once on a time I used to be
The Patriarch Abraham's pet Flea,
Over his heart he nourished me,
    Hip, hop!
Often he thrust his hairy phiz
And most remarkable proboscis
Into his breast for conferences,
    Hip, hip, hip! Hop, hop!

Quoth Abraham, 'Full well I wot
I labour, wife, but you do not.
How shall I get a son, old trot?'
    Hip, hop!
Snapped Sarah, 'La!—take my advice:
Go ask that Flea you find so nice,
Do what he bids you and don't think twice.'
    Hip, hip, hip! Hop, hop!

'Come, little comrade, what do you bid?'
Said I, 'I marked, while you two chid,
One who kept half a smile hid.'
    Hip, hop!
Then Abraham, 'What? why? When? who?'
And I, 'I'll tell, if what you do
And where you go, your Flea may too.'
    Hip, hip, hip! Hop, hop!

'Come, Little Friend, proceed, proceed;
My case is very hard indeed—'
Chirped I, 'Abe, did you never heed,
    Hip, hop!

ROBERT NICHOLS

How softly Hagar's eyelids sink
When by your bed she pours your drink?' ...
The Patriarch gave a mighty wink,
    Hip, hip, hip! Hop, hop!

Then 'Ha-ha-ha! and Ho-ho-ho!
Bravo, my Little Friend, bravo!
Hop-skip-and-jump and away-we-go!'
    Hip, hop!
All night in Paradise I dwelt,
How dainty sweet each arbour smelled,
The things I saw! The things I felt!
    Hip, hip, hip! Hop, hop!

NORMAN NICHOLSON

CLEATOR MOOR

From one shaft at Cleator Moor
They mined for coal and iron ore.
This harvest below ground could show
Black and red currants on one tree.

In furnaces they burnt the coal,
The ore was smelted into steel,
And railway lines from end to end
Corseted the bulging land.

Pylons sprouted on the fells,
Stakes were driven in like nails,
And the ploughed fields of Devonshire
Were sliced with the steel of Cleator Moor.

The land waxed fat and greedy too,
It would not share the fruits it grew,
And coal and ore, as sloe and plum,
Lay black and red for jamming time.

The pylons rusted on the fells,
The gutters leaked beside the walls,
And women searched the ebb-tide tracks
For knobs of coal or broken sticks.

But now the pits are wick with men,
Digging like dogs dig for a bone:
For food and life *we* dig the earth—
In Cleator Moor they dig for death.

Every waggon of cold coal
Is fire to drive a turbine wheel;
Every knuckle of soft ore
A bullet in a soldier's ear.

The miner at the rockface stands,
With his segged and bleeding hands
Heaps on his head the fiery coal,
And feels the iron in his soul.

SONG AT NIGHT

'Music for a while'
Make audible the smile
   That eyes no longer see;
With crying crayon write
Across the unhearing night
   The shape of sighs for me.

Music for a time
Resolve the brawls of rhyme
   That chord within my head;
Sweet as starlight, shine,
Illuminate the line,
   Setting the word unsaid.

When Dryden's page is bare,
And silent Purcell's air,
   And mute the singing sky,
Then let me pluck one name
And echo clear proclaim
   Not I, my dear, not I.

CAEDMON

NORMAN NICHOLSON

Above me the abbey, grey arches on the cliff,
The lights lit in the nave, pale prayers against the night,
For still the Blessed Hilda burns like a brand
Among the black thorns, the thickets of darkness,
The ways and walls of a wild land,
Where the spade grates on stone, on the grappling gorse,
And the Norse gods clamber on the Christian crosses.
Below me the sea, the angry, the hungered,
Gnashing the grey chalk, grinding the cobbles.
The snow falls like feathers, the hail like quills,
The sun sets, and the night rises like a sea-mist,
And the fog is in the bones of the drowned. Here fare far out
Mariners and marauders, foragers and fishermen.
Tearing their treasure from the teeth of the waves, from the gullet of the gaping shores—
Over the heaped and heaving hills they return to the wistful harbours,
The freeman's blood and the sea's salt frozen on the gold.
Honour to warriors and wanderers, honour to the wise,
Honour to kings and kinsmen of kings, honour to councillors,
Honour to priests, honour to pilgrims,
Honour even to minstrels, the many-songed migrants.
But never have I ventured forth, neither on the northern tides,
Nor more than a shin's depth down the steep and staggering shore;

NORMAN NICHOLSON

I have not roamed with the fighting men nor fired the Scotsmen's byres.
Yet I, even I, have heard the angels speak,
I, who never learned the liturgical tongue,
Who cannot read the written revelation,
Walking at night on the shingle, waking at dawn in the straw,
I have seen long spears of lightning lance at my eyes,
And felt the words, pricked out with fire,
Notched in my bones and burning in my body.
The angels crawled like gold lice through my dreams.
By the grey sea, under the grimacing clouds,
I hack and hammer at the handiwork of verse,
Feeling the sting of words, fearing the angels' threats,
Hoping that when the tide is full I may seek my unhaunted bed.

WILFRED OWEN

SHADWELL STAIR

I am the ghost of Shadwell Stair.
   Along the wharves by the water-house,
   And through the dripping slaughter-house,
I am the shadow that walks there.

Yet I have flesh both firm and cool,
   And eyes tumultuous as the gems
   Of moons and lamps in the lapping Thames
When dusk sails wavering down the pool.

Shuddering the purple street-arc burns
   Where I watch always; from the banks
   Dolorously the shipping clanks,
And after me a strange tide turns.

I walk till the stars of London wane
   And dawn creeps up the Shadwell Stair.
   But when the crowing syrens blare
I with another ghost am lain.

INSENSIBILITY

I

Happy are men who yet before they are killed
Can let their veins run cold.
Whom no compassion fleers
Or makes their feet
Sore on the alleys cobbled with their brothers.

Wilfred The front line withers,
Owen But they are troops who fade, not flowers
For poets' tearful fooling:
Men, gaps for filling:
Losses who might have fought
Longer; but no one bothers.

II

And some cease feeling
Even themselves or for themselves.
Dullness best solves
The tease and doubt of shelling,
And Chance's strange arithmetic
Comes simpler than the reckoning of their shilling.
They keep no check on armies' decimation.

III

Happy are these who lose imagination:
They have enough to carry with ammunition.
Their spirit drags no pack,
Their old wounds save with cold can not more ache.
Having seen all things red,
Their eyes are rid
Of the hurt of the colour of blood for ever.
And terror's first constriction over,
Their hearts remain small-drawn.
Their senses in some scorching cautery of battle
Now long since ironed,
Can laugh among the dying, unconcerned.

IV

Happy the soldier home, with not a notion
How somewhere, every dawn, some men attack,
And many sighs are drained.
Happy the lad whose mind was never trained:

His days are worth forgetting more than not.   **WILFRED**
He sings along the march   **OWEN**
Which we march taciturn, because of dusk,
The long, forlorn, relentless trend
From larger day to huger night.

V

We wise, who with a thought besmirch
Blood over all our soul,
How should we see our task
But through his blunt and lashless eyes?
Alive, he is not vital overmuch;
Dying, not mortal overmuch;
Nor sad, nor proud,
Nor curious at all.
He cannot tell
Old men's placidity from his.

VI

But cursed are dullards whom no cannon stuns,
That they should be as stones;
Wretched are they, and mean
With paucity that never was simplicity.
By choice they made themselves immune
To pity and whatever moans in man
Before the last sea and the hapless stars;
Whatever mourns when many leave these shores;
Whatever shares
The eternal reciprocity of tears.

DULCE ET DECORUM EST

WILFRED OWEN

Bent double, like old beggars under sacks,
Knock-kneed, coughing like hags, we cursed through sludge,
Till on the haunting flares we turned our backs,
And towards our distant rest began to trudge.
Men marched asleep. Many had lost their boots,
But limped on, blood-shod. All went lame, all blind;
Drunk with fatigue; deaf even to the hoots
Of gas-shells dropping softly behind.

Gas! GAS! Quick, boys!—An ecstasy of fumbling,
Fitting the clumsy helmets just in time,
But someone still was yelling out and stumbling
And floundering like a man in fire or lime.—
Dim through the misty panes and thick green light,
As under a green sea, I saw him drowning.

In all my dreams before my helpless sight
He plunges at me, guttering, choking, drowning.

If in some smothering dreams, you too could pace
Behind the wagon that we flung him in,
And watch the white eyes writhing in his face,
His hanging face, like a devil's sick of sin;
If you could hear, at every jolt, the blood
Come gargling from the froth-corrupted lungs,
Bitter as the cud
Of vile, incurable sores on innocent tongues,—
My friend, you would not tell with such high zest
To children ardent for some desperate glory,
The old Lie: Dulce et decorum est
Pro patria mori.

HERBERT PALMER

THE WOUNDED HAWK

I have with fishing-rod and line
    Roved many banks and had great play;
But there are shadows in my mind,
    And one will stick till dying day.

I saw one morn near Muker bridge,
    Beside the wood I sought to pass,
A great hawk—crippled in the wing—
    Spread wide and struggling on the grass—

Shot by some keeper as it flew
    In cruel ecstasy of Spring.
It was of strange and mottled hue—
    A crag-land, evil, splendid thing,

Of crookéd beak and claws like steel;
    The wood danced jigs if it knew aught.
'But can the smaller creatures feel
    As you appear to feel?' I thought.

Such anguish filled each great round eye
    It wrung my heart and rocked my brain;
I longed for powers within the Sky
    To give it strength to fly again—

To soar and swoop and hunt and prey,
    Fulfil its nature to the core;
The sunlight seemed to leave the day;
    Upon my joy there closed a door.

HERBERT PALMER

It glared at me in fear and pain,
    Then beat its wings and strove to fly.
I stopped awhile, but could not aid;
    Then thought, as I went slowly by—

We're pages from the self-same book;
    But you—you're done. I wait God's wish.
One hunts with beak, and one with hook,
    And one with word—birds, knaves, fools, fish.

AUNT ZILLAH SPEAKS

I never look upon the sea
And hear its waves sighing,
But I must get me home again
To still my heart's wild crying.
All my years like drowned sailors,
All my days that used to be,
Seem drifting in the silver spray
And mourning by the sea.

But when I take a holiday
I go where flowers are growing,
Where thrushes sing and skylarks wing
And happy streams are flowing;
And the great hills clothed with bracken,
As far as I would flee,
Fling their towering crests to the stars on high
To shield me from the sea.

RUTH PITTER

THE MILITARY HARPIST

Strangely assorted, the shape of song and the bloody man.

Under the harp's gilt shoulder and rainlike strings,
Prawn-eyed, with prawnlike bristle, well-waxed moustache,
With long tight cavalry legs, and the spurred boot
Ready upon the swell, the Old Sweat waits.

Now dies, and dies hard, the stupid, well-relished fortissimo,
Wood-wind alone inviting the liquid tone,
The voice of the holy and uncontending, the harp.

Ceasing to ruminate interracial fornications,
He raises his hands, and his wicked old mug is David's,
Pastoral, rapt, the king and the poet in innocence,
Singing Saul in himself asleep, and the ancient Devil
Clean out of countenance, as with an army of angels.

He is now where his bunion has no existence.
Breathing an atmosphere free of pipeclay and swearing,
He wears the starched nightshirt of the hereafter, his halo
Is plain manly brass with a permanent polish,
Requiring no oily rag and no Soldier's Friend.

RUTH His place is with the beloved poet of Israel,
PITTER With the wandering minnesinger and the loves of
      Provence,
    With Blondel footsore and heartsore, the voice in the
      darkness
    Crying like beauty bereaved beneath many a donjon,
    O Richard! O king! where is the lion of England!

    With Howell, Llewellyn, and far in the feral north
    With the savage fame of the hero in glen and in ben,
    At the morning discourse of saints in the island Eire,
    And at nameless doings in the stone-circle, the
      dreadful grove.

    Thus far into the dark do I delve for his likeness:
    He harps at the Druid sacrifice, where the golden
      string
    Sings to the golden knife and the victim's shriek.

    Strangely assorted, the shape of song and the bloody
      man.

THE TIGRESS

The raging and the ravenous,
The nocturnal terror in gold,
Red-fire-coated, green-fire-eyed.
The fanged, the clawed, the frightful leaper.
Great-sinewed, silent walker,
Tyrant of all the timid, the implacable
Devil of slaughter, the she-demon
Matchless in fury, matchless love
Gives her whelps in the wildernesses.
Clearing the stains of slaughter
From her jaws with tongue and forearm,

She licks her young and suckles them
Delicately as a doe:
She blood-glutted is the angel
To their blindness, she is minister
Between life and these feeble young
In barren places, where no help is.

Or man-imprisoned often disdaining
To rear her royal brood, though cheated
Into bearing, she abandons
All at birth, and bids them die.
Utter love and utter hatred
Cannot compromise; she gives
Her whole being to their being
Or rejects them into death.

No thought intervenes; her justice
Is not mind-perverted: O tigress,
Royal mother without pity,
Could but one thought arise within
That greatly-sculptured skull, behind
The phosphorus-eyes compunction burn,
Well might it be for all these millions
Mind-infected, mother-betrayed:
No beast so hapless as a man.

THE VIPER

Barefoot I went and made no sound;
The earth was hot beneath:
The air was quivering around,
The circling kestrel eyed the ground
And hung above the heath.

RUTH PITTER

There in the pathway stretched along
The lovely serpent lay:
She reared not up the heath among,
She bowed her head, she sheathed her tongue,
And shining stole away.

Fair was the brave embroidered dress,
Fairer the gold eyes shone:
Loving her not, yet did I bless
The fallen angel's comeliness;
And gazed when she had gone.

BUT FOR LUST

But for lust we could be friends,
   On each other's necks could weep:
In each other's arms could sleep
   In the calm the cradle lends:

Lends awhile, and takes away.
   But for hunger, but for fear,
Calm could be our day and year
   From the yellow to the grey:

From the gold to the grey hair,
   But for passion we could rest,
But for passion we could feast
   On compassion everywhere.

Even in this night I know
   By the awful living dead,
By this craving tear I shed,
   Somewhere, somewhere it is **so**.

WILLIAM PLOMER

MEWS FLAT MONA
A Memory of the 'Twenties

She flourished in the 'Twenties, 'hectic' days of Peace,
'Twas good to be alive then, and to be a Baronet's
    Niece.
> *Oh, Mona! it's not so good now!*

Mona in the last war was a Problem Child,
She roared and ranted, so they let her run wild;
Expelled from St. Faith's, she was shot from a gun
At a circus she'd joined, for a bet, at Lausanne.
> *Oh, Mona! they're rid of you now!*

She had her hair bobbed, when the fashion began,
To catch the eye of some soft-hearted man.
> *Oh, Mona! they're just as soft now!*

A man was caught; she ran off in her teens
With the heir to a fortune from adding-machines,
But he failed to reckon up the wear and tear,
By the time she left him he had iron-grey hair.
> *Oh, Mona! you're subtracted now!*

Mona took a flat in a Mayfair Mews;
To do that then was to be in the news.
> *Oh, Mona! it wouldn't be now!*

The walls were of glass and the floor of pewter,
This was thought 'intriguing', but the bathroom was
    cuter;

WILLIAM On a sofa upholstered in human skin
PLOMER Mona did researches in original sin.
   Oh, Mona! they're concluded now!

Mews Flat Mona, as a Bright Young Thing,
Led a pet crocodile about on a string;
In a green cloche hat and a knee-length skirt
She dragged the tired reptile till it was inert.
   Oh, Mona! it's gone to earth now!

Diamond bracelets blazed on her wrists
(They were not presented by misogynists)
And Mona got engaged to a scatterbrained peer,
His breach of promise cost him pretty dear.
   Oh, Mona! he couldn't pay now!

When she gave a dance she engaged three bands,
And she entered the Ritz once walking on her hands,
She drove round London in a crimson Rolls,
'The soul of every party'—as if parties had souls!
   Oh, Mona! the party's over now!

Mews Flat Mona, as a Period Vamp,
Spent a week-end in a nudist camp;
Her barefaced behaviour upset the crowd
And she came back sunburnt under a cloud.
   Oh, Mona! you're in the shade now!

She babbled of Coué and also of Freud,
But her book of engagements was the one she enjoyed.
   Oh, Mona! you've no dates now!

She lived for a time with an Irish Jew
And thought it an 'amusing' thing to do;

He taught her to take morphia, heroin, and 'snow', WILLIAM
A giddy life, but she was used to vertigo. PLOMER
    Oh, Mona! no pipe-dreams now!

Too bright were her eyes, the pace was too fast,
Both ends of the candle were burnt out at last.
    Oh, Mona! you're blacked out now!

She stepped from the top of an Oxford Street store;
She might well have waited a split second more
For she fell like a bomb on an elderly curate
And his life was over before he could insure it.
    Oh, Mona! you're exploded now!

When they came with a shovel to shift her remains
They found a big heart but no vestige of brains.
    Oh, Mona! that accounts for you now!

FOR MY FATHER

I think a time will come when you will understand
That I was forced to try and fly and learn to sing
And that because I fell, echoless, between dark rocks
Is of itself no proof that if I had not run away
I would have grown strong and added to
The long tradition of you and your quiet sires.
Remember too, that this emigrating is of itself
Part of your own long silent heritage.
Else, how sir, did you come to be American?

THE MUSE TO AN UNKNOWN POET

I wonder poet, can you take it
Alone out there among the hireling men.
The dawn, if ever there is to be a dawn
Must come, long after you are gone.
There is no love, no laughter, no parades,
And mighty little ham and eggs,
Alone out there among the hireling men.

EZRA POUND

THE SEAFARER

From the Anglo-Saxon

May I for my own self song's truth reckon,
Journey's jargon, how I in harsh days
Hardship endured oft.
Bitter breast-cares have I abided,
Known on my keel many a care's hold,
And dire sea-surge, and there I oft spent
Narrow nightwatch nigh the ship's head
While she tossed close to cliffs. Coldly afflicted,
My feet were by frost benumbed.
Chill its chains are; chafing sighs
Hew my heart round and hunger begot
Mere-weary mood. Lest man know not
That he on dry land loveliest liveth,
List how I, care-wretched, on ice-cold sea,
Weathered the winter, wretched outcast
Deprived of my kinsmen;
Hung with hard ice-flakes, where hail-scur flew,
There I heard naught save the harsh sea
And ice-cold wave, at whiles the swan cries,
Did for my games the gannet's clamour,
Sea-fowls' loudness was for me laughter,
The mews' singing all my mead-drink.
Storms, on the stone-cliffs beaten, fell on the stern
In icy feathers; full oft the eagle screamed
With spray on his pinion.
                        Not any protector
May make merry man faring needy.
This he little believes, who aye in winsome life

EZRA POUND

Abides 'mid burghers some heavy business,
Wealthy and wine-flushed, how I weary oft
Must bide above brine.
Neareth nightshade, snoweth from north,
Frost froze the land, hail fell on earth then,
Corn of the coldest. Nathless there knocketh now
The heart's thought that I on high streams
The salt-wavy tumult traverse alone.
Moaneth alway my mind's lust
That I fare forth, that I afar hence
Seek out a foreign fastness.
For this there's no mood-lofty man over earth's midst
Not though he be given his good, but will have in his youth greed;
Nor his deed to the daring, nor his king to the faithful
But shall have his sorrow for sea-fare
Whatever his lord will.
He hath not heart for harping, nor in ring-having
Nor winsomeness to wife, nor world's delight
Nor any whit else save the wave's slash,
Yet longing comes on him to fare forth on the water.
Bosque taketh blossom, comes beauty of berries,
Fields to fairness, land fares brisker,
All this admonisheth man eager of mood,
The heart turns to travel so that he then thinks
On flood-ways to be far departing.
Cuckoo calleth with gloomy crying,
He singeth summerward, bodeth sorrow,
The bitter heart's blood. Burgher knows not—
He the prosperous man—what some perform
Where wandering them widest draweth,
So that but now my heart burst from my breastlock,
My mood 'mid the mere-flood,
Over the whale's acre, would wander wide.

On earth's shelter cometh oft to me,
Eager and ready, the crying lone-flyer,
Whets for the whale-path the heart irresistibly,
O'er tracks of ocean; seeing that anyhow
My lord deems to me this dead life
On loan and on land, I believe not
That any earth-weal eternal standeth
Save there be somewhat calamitous
That, ere a man's tide go, turn it to twain
Disease or oldness or sword-hate
Beats out the breath from a doom-gripped body.
And for this, every earl whatever, for those speaking
    after—
Laud of the living, boasteth some last word,
That he will work ere he pass onward,
Frame on the fair earth 'gainst foes his malice,
Daring ado, . . .
So that all men shall honour him after
And his laud beyond them remain 'mid the English,
Aye, for ever, a lasting life's-blast,
Delight 'mid the doughty.
                   Days little durable,
And all arrogance of earthen riches,
There come now no kings nor Caesars
Nor gold-giving lords like those gone.
Howe'er in mirth most magnified,
Whoe'er in life lived most lordliest,
Drear all this excellence, delights undurable!
Waneth the watch, but the world holdeth.
Tomb hideth trouble. The blade is layed low.
Earthly glory ageth and seareth.
No man at all going the earth's gait,
But age fares against him, his face paleth,
Grey-haired he groaneth, knows gone companions,
Lordly men, are to earth o'er given,

Nor may he then the flesh-cover, whose life ceaseth,
Nor eat the sweet nor feel the sorry,
Nor stir hand nor think in mid heart,
And though he strew the grave with gold,
His born brothers, their buried bodies
Be an unlikely treasure hoard.

SESTINA: ALTAFORTE

Loquitur: *En* Bertrans de Born.
    Dante Alighieri put this man in hell for that he was a stirrer up of strife.
    Eccovi!
    Judge ye!
    Have I dug him up again?
The scene is at his castle, Altaforte. 'Papiols' is his jongleur. 'The Leopard', the *device* of Richard Coeur de Lion.

I

Damn it all! all this our South stinks peace.
You whoreson dog, Papiols, come! Let's to music!
I have no life save when the swords clash.
But ah! when I see the standards gold, vair, purple, opposing
And the broad fields beneath them turn crimson,
Then howls my heart nigh mad with rejoicing.

II

In hot summer have I great rejoicing
When the tempests kill the earth's foul peace,
And the lightnings from black heav'n flash crimson,
And the fierce thunders roar me their music

And the winds shriek through the clouds mad,
    opposing,
And through all the riven skies God's swords clash.

III

Hell grant soon we hear again the swords clash!
And the shrill neighs of destriers in battle rejoicing,
Spiked breast to spiked breast opposing!
Better one hour's stour than a year's peace
With fat boards, bawds, wine and frail music!
Bah! there's no wine like the blood's crimson!

IV

And I love to see the sun rise blood-crimson.
And I watch his spears through the dark clash
And it fills all my heart with rejoicing
And pries wide my mouth with fast music
When I see him so scorn and defy peace,
His lone might 'gainst all darkness opposing.

V

The man who fears war and squats opposing
My words for stour, hath no blood of crimson
But is fit only to rot in womanish peace
Far from where worth's won and the swords clash
For the death of such sluts I go rejoicing;
Yea, I fill all the air with my music.

VI

Papiols, Papiols, to the music!
There's no sound like to swords swords opposing,
No cry like the battle's rejoicing
When our elbows and swords drip the crimson

EZRA POUND

And our charges 'gainst 'The Leopard's' rush clash.
May God damn for ever all who cry 'Peace!'

VII

And let the music of the swords make them crimson!
Hell grant soon we hear again the swords clash!
Hell blot black for alway the thought 'Peace'!

PHYLLIDULA

Phyllidula is scrawny but amorous,
Thus have the gods awarded her,
That in pleasure she receives more than she can give;
If she does not count this blessed
Let her change her religion.

THE FAUN

Ha! sir, I have seen you sniffing and snoozling about
 among my flowers.
And what do you know about horticulture, you
 capriped?
'Come, Auster, come Apeliota,
And see the faun in our garden.
But if you move or speak
This thing will run at you
And scare itself to spasms.'

From THE PISAN CANTOS   EZRA POUND

Tudor indeed is gone and every rose,
Blood-red, blanch-white that in the sunset glows
Cries: 'Blood, Blood, Blood!' against the gothic stone
Of England, as the Howard or Boleyn knows.

Nor seeks the carmine petal to infer;
Nor is the white bud Time's inquisitor
Probing to know if its new-gnarled root
Twists from York's head or belly of Lancaster;

Or if a rational soul should stir, perchance,
Within the stem or summer shoot to advance
Contrition's utmost throw, seeking in thee
But oblivion, not thy forgiveness, FRANCE.

From THE PISAN CANTOS

What thou lovest well remains,
                              the rest is dross
What thou lov'st well shall not be reft from thee
What thou lov'st well is thy true heritage
Whose world, or mine or theirs
                              or is it of none?
First came the seen, then thus the palpable
    Elysium, though it were in the halls of hell,
What thou lovest well is thy true heritage
What thou lov'st well shall not be reft from thee

EZRA POUND

The ant's a centaur in his dragon world.
Pull down thy vanity, it is not man
Made courage, or made order, or made grace,
    Pull down thy vanity, I say pull down.
Learn of the green world what can be thy place
In scaled invention or true artistry,
Pull down thy vanity,
                    Paquin pull down!
The green casque has outdone your elegance.

'Master thyself, then others shall thee beare'
    Pull down thy vanity
Thou art a beaten dog beneath the hail,
A swollen magpie in a fitful sun,
Half black half white
Nor knowst'ou wing from tail
Pull down thy vanity
    How mean thy hates
Fostered in falsity,
    Pull down thy vanity,
Rathe to destroy, niggard in charity,
Pull down thy vanity,
    I say pull down.

But to have done instead of not doing
    this is not vanity
To have, with decency, knocked
That a Blunt should open
    To have gathered from the air a live tradition
or from a fine old eye the unconquered flame
This is not vanity.
    Here error is all in the not done,
all in the diffidence that faltered.

F. T. PRINCE

THE TOKEN

More beautiful than any gift you gave
You were, a child so beautiful as to seem
To promise ruin what no child can have
Or woman give. And so a Roman gem
I choose to be your token: here a laurel
Springs to its young height, hangs a broken limb.
And here a group of women wanly quarrel
At a sale of Cupids. A hawk looks at them.

KATHLEEN RAINE

WORRY ABOUT MONEY

Wearing worry about money like a hair shirt
I lie down in my bed and wrestle with my angel.
My bank-manager could not sanction my continuance
 for another day,
But life itself wakes me each morning, and love

Urges me to give although I have no money
In the bank at this moment and ought properly
To cease to exist in a world where poverty
Is a shameful and ridiculous offence.

Having no one to advise me, I open the Bible
And shut my eyes and put my finger on a text
And read that the widow with the young son
Must give first to the prophetic genius
From the little there is in the bin of flour and the
 cruse of oil.

HERBERT READ

THE WHITE ISLE OF LEUCE

Leave Helen to her lover. Draw away
before the sea is dark. Frighten with your oars
the white sea-birds till they rise
on wings that veer
against the black sentinels
    of the silent wood.

The oars beat off; Achilles cannot see
the prows that dip against the dim shore's line.
But the rowers as they rest on the lifting waves
hear the revelry of Helen and a voice singing
of battle and love. The rowers hear and rest
and tremble for the limbs of Helen and the secrets of
    the sacred isle.

SIC ET NON

I. THE COMPLAINT OF HELOISE

Elle a aussi cette chose en sextant de marine.
—ANTONIN ARTAUD

    Abelard was: God is
      my love, I his
    learned lass. But God is
      not near.

    Abelard my lover
      was. I felt the
    lusts that burnt us were
      too sweet:

I feared they could not last.
   I saw them pass
shedding brands to harass
   my life.

They went: cruelly forc'd.
   That he should know
doom of flesh, unique loss!
   Dear me!

I could show a white face,
   a pious dress;
but very flowers in my breast
   all fresh.

Pluck them. God pluck them. I
   plucked them madly.
But ever burgeon'd rose,
   lily:

All the emblems
   of my distress.
God help me to hide them
   now.

II. THE PORTRAIT OF ABELARD

The wild boars are grubbing for acorns
Among the moist fallen leaves,
And the Arudzon disperses
Mist along its course.
The Paraclete is cold;
   the cloisters comfortless.

HERBERT READ

The eunuch is contrite;
His genitals are gone to dust—
Like amputated limbs are burnt
These twenty years in acid earth.
The river runs
   along the horizontal light.

His mind is foster'd on the infinite;
His voice is gentle, animate
With intellectual faith.
The flowers toss
   against his moving feet.

The body when depriv'd of lust
Offers to an outer God
Its forced immaculation.
The scaly sky
   hath cast its glittering sheath.

And now the illumination of the stars
Visits with raw radiance
The body's hollow cave.
There bounds the fleshy sphere
More playfully
   sapp'd of seminal rheum.

From MUTATIONS OF THE PHOENIX

Phoenix, bird of terrible pride,
ruddy eye and iron beak!
Come, leave the incinerary nest;
spread your red wings.

HERBERT READ

And soaring in the golden light
survey the world;
hover against the highest sky;
menace men with your strange phenomena.

For a haunt seek a coign
in a rocky land;
when the night is black
settle on the bleak headlands.

Utter shrill warnings in the cold dawn sky;
let them descend
into the shutter'd minds below you
Inhabit our wither'd nerves.

EDGELL RICKWORD

COSMOGONY

Cosmic Leviathan, that monstrous fish,
stirred in his ancient sleep, begins to dream;
and out of nothingness dishevelled suns
crawl, with live planets tangled in their hair.

And through the valleys of those phantom worlds
some pursue shadows painfully and grasp
the husks they see, and name one Rose, and one
Willow, that leans and whispers over pools.

They speak of mountains reared and crashing seas
and forests that seem older than the hills;
or meet a maiden-shade and plan with her
sojourn and rapture in Eternity.

Slowly the sunrise breaks beyond those hills,
by waveless seas; and in the golden light,
heavy with his long sleep Leviathan
splashes, and half recalls a waking dream.

THE CASCADE

Lovers may find similitudes
to the sweet babbling girlish noise,
in the inhuman crystal voice
that calls from mountain solitudes;

EDGELL RICK-WORD

as that's but movement overlaid
with water, a faint shining thought,
spirit is to music wrought
in the swift passion of a maid.

It is her body sings so clear,
chanting in the woods of night;
on Earth's dark precipice a white
Prometheus, bound like water here;

the eager Joys toward their task
from dusky veins beat up in flocks,
but still her curious patience mocks
the consummation lovers ask.

Lying on ferns she seems to wear
(the silver tissue of the skin
radiant from the fire within)
light as her weed and shade for hair;

rapt in communion so intense
the nicer senses fail and she,
sweet Phoenix, burns on Pain's rich tree
in praise and prayer and frankincense.

The iron beaks that seek her flesh
vex more her lovers' anxious minds,
in whose dim glades each hunter finds
his own torn spirit in the mesh.

ANNE RIDLER

CHRISTMAS AND COMMON BIRTH

Christmas declares the glory of the flesh:
And therefore a European might wish
To celebrate it not in midwinter but in spring,
When physical life is strong,
When the consent to live is forced even on the young,
Juice is in the soil, the leaf, the vein,
Sugar flows to movement in limbs and brain.
Also, before a birth, in nourishing the child,
We turn again to the earth
With unusual longing—to what is rich, wild,
Substantial: scents that have been stored and
    strengthened
In apple lofts, the underwash of woods, and in barns;
Drawn through the lengthened root; pungent in
    cones
(While the fir wood stands waiting; the beech wood
    aspiring,
Each in a different silence), and breaking out in
    spring
With scent sight sound indivisible in song.

Yet if you think again
It is good that Christmas comes at the dark dream of
    the year
That might wish to sleep for ever.

For birth is awaking, birth is effort and pain;
And now at midwinter are the hints, inklings
(Sodden primrose, honeysuckle greening)
That sleep must be broken.
To bear new life or learn to live is an exacting joy:

ANNE The whole self must waken; you cannot predict the
RIDLER   way
It will happen, or master the responses beforehand.
For any birth makes an inconvenient demand;
Like all holy things
It is frequently a nuisance, and its needs never end;
Strange freedom it brings: we should welcome release
From its long merciless rehearsal of peace.

   So Christ comes
At the iron senseless time, comes
To force the glory into frozen veins:
   His warmth wakes
Green life glazed in the pool, wakes
All calm and crystal trance with living pains.

   And each year
In seasonal growth is good—year
That lacking love is a stale story at best;
   By God's birth
All common birth is holy; birth
Is all at Christmas time and wholly blest.

NOW PHILIPPA IS GONE

Now Philippa is gone, that so divinely
Could strum and sing, and is rufus and gay,
Have we the heart to sing, or at midday
Dive under Trotton Bridge? We shall only
Doze in the yellow spikenard by the wood
And take our tea and melons in the shade.

W. R. RODGERS

BEAGLES

Over rock and wrinkled ground
Ran the lingering nose of hound,
The little and elastic hare
Stretched herself nor stayed to stare.

Stretched herself, and far away
Darted through the chinks of day,
Behind her, shouting out her name,
The whole blind world galloping came.

Over hills a running line
Curled like a whip-lash, fast and fine,
Past me sailed the sudden pack
Along the taut and tingling track.

From the far flat scene each shout
Like jig-saw piece came tumbling out,
I took and put them all together
And then they turned into a tether.

A tether that held me to the hare
Here, there and everywhere.

CAROL

Deep in the fading leaves of light
There lay the flower that darkness knows,
Till winter stripped and brought to light
The most incomparable Rose
That blows, that blows.

W. R. RODGERS

The flashing mirrors of the snow
Keep turning and returning still:
To see the lovely child below
And hold him is their only will;
Keep still, keep still.

And to let go his very cry
The clinging echoes are so slow
That still his wail they multiply
Though he lie singing now below,
So low, so low.

Even the doves forget to grieve
And gravely to his greeting fly
And the lone places that they leave
All follow and are standing by
On high, on high.

ISAAC ROSENBERG

THE IMMORTALS

I killed them, but they would not die.
Yea! all the day and all the night
For them I could not rest nor sleep,
Nor guard from them nor hide in flight.

Then in my agony I turned
And made my hands red in their gore.
In vain—for faster than I slew
They rose more cruel than before.

I killed and killed with slaughter mad;
I killed till all my strength was gone.
And still they rose to torture me,
For Devils only die for fun.

I used to think the Devil hid
In women's smiles and wine's carouse.
I called him Satan, Beelzebub.
But now I call him dirty louse.

THE FEMALE GOD

We curl into your eyes—
They drink our fires and have never
    drained.
In the fierce forest of your hair
Our desires beat blindly for their treasure.

In your eyes' subtle pit,
Far down, glimmer our souls.
And your hair like massive forest trees
Shadows our pulses, overtired and dumb.

ISAAC ROSENBERG

Like a candle lost in an electric glare
Our spirits tread your eyes' infinities.
In the wrecking waves of your tumultuous locks
Do you not hear the moaning of our pulses?

Queen! Goddess! Animal!

In sleep do your dreams battle with our souls?
When your hair is spread like a lover on the pillow
Do not our jealous pulses wake between?

You have dethroned the ancient God,
You have usurped his Sabbath, his common days,
Yea! every moment is delivered to you,
Our Temple, our Eternal, our one God.

Our souls have passed into your eyes,
Our days into your hair,
And you, our rose-deaf prison, are very pleased with the world,
Your world.

SIEGFRIED SASSOON

IN BARRACKS

The barrack-square, washed clean with rain,
Shines wet and wintry-grey and cold.
Young Fusiliers, strong-legged and bold,
March and wheel and march again.
The sun looks over the barrack gate,
Warm and white with glaring shine,
To watch the soldiers of the Line
That life has hired to fight with fate.

Fall out; the long parades are done.
Up comes the dark; down goes the sun.
The square is walled with windowed light.
Sleep well, you lusty Fusiliers;
Shut your brave eyes on sense and sight,
And banish from your dreamless ears
The bugle's dying notes that say,
'Another night; another day.'

STAND-TO: GOOD FRIDAY MORNING

I'd been on duty from two till four.
I went and stared at the dug-out door.
Down in the frowst I heard them snore.
'Stand to!' Somebody grunted and swore.
    Dawn was misty; the skies were still;
    Larks were singing, discordant, shrill;
    They seemed happy; but I felt ill.

SIEG-　　　Deep in water I splashed my way
FRIED　　　Up the trench to our bogged front line.
SASSOON　　Rain had fallen the whole damned night.
　　　　　　O Jesus, send me a wound today,
　　　　　　And I'll believe in Your bread and wine,
　　　　　　And get my bloody old sins washed white!

'BLIGHTERS'

The House is crammed: tier beyond tier they grin
And cackle at the Show, while prancing ranks
Of harlots shrill the chorus, drunk with din;
'We're sure the Kaiser loves our dear old Tanks!'

I'd like to see a Tank come down the Stalls,
Lurching to rag-time tunes, or 'Home, sweet Home',
And there'd be no more jokes in Music-halls
To mock the riddled corpses round Bapaume.

MONODY ON THE DEMOLITION OF DEVONSHIRE HOUSE

Strolling one afternoon along a street
Whose valuable vastness can compare
With anything on earth in the complete
Efficiency of its mammoniac air—
Strolling (to put it plainly) through those bits
Of Londonment adjacent to the Ritz
(While musing on the social gap between
Myself, whose arrogance is mostly brainy,
And those whose pride, on sunlit days and rainy,
Must loll and glide in yacht and limousine),
Something I saw, beyond a boarded barrier,
Which manifested well that Time's no tarrier.

Where stood the low-built mansion, once so great,   SIEG-
Ducal, demure, secure in its estate—   FRIED
Where Byron rang the bell and limped upstairs,   SASSOON
And Lord knows what political affairs
Got muddled and remodelled while Their Graces
Manned unperturbed Elizabethan faces—
There, blankly overlooked by wintry strange
Frontage of houses rawly-lit by change,
Industrious workmen reconstructed quite
The lumbered, pegged, and excavated site;
And not one nook survived to screen a mouse
In what was Devonshire (God rest it) House.

EARLY CHRONOLOGY

Slowly the daylight left our listening faces.

Professor Brown with level baritone
Discoursed into the dusk.
                 Five thousand years
He guided us through scientific spaces
Of excavated History; till his lone
Roads of research grew blurred; and in our ears
Time was the rumoured tongues of vanished races,
And Thought a chartless Age of Ice and Stone.

The story ended: and the darkened air
Flowered while he lit his pipe; an aureole glowed
Enwreathed with smoke: the moment's match-light
    showed
His rosy face, broad brow, and smooth grey hair,
Backed by the crowded book-shelves.
                      In his wake

SIEG-　An archaeologist began to make
FRIED　Assumptions about aqueducts (he quoted
SASSOON　Professor Sandstorm's book); and soon they floated
　　　　Through desiccated forests; mangled myths;
　　　　And argued easily round megaliths.

　　　　Beyond the college garden something glinted;
　　　　A copper moon climbed clear above black trees.
　　　　Some Lydian coin? ... Professor Brown agrees
　　　　That copper coins *were* in that Culture minted.
　　　　But, as her whitening way aloft she took,
　　　　I thought she had a pre-dynastic look.

MARTIN SEYMOUR-SMITH

HE CAME TO VISIT ME

He came to visit me, my mortal messenger.
    I saw the sorrow stamped upon his face.
He bade me chide at him, for grief. 'But sir'
    I said, 'you know your dominating place.'

'That's it,' he said to me, 'you spin the thread
    Of life in me; you make me flesh and blood,
Although we both wish now that I were dead.
    This sorrow on my face is but a hood;

Behind there is a blank white wall of skin—
    An eyeless, mouthless, noseless face: neutrality.
It is dark death that lives behind the thin
    Pale flesh. You have my eyes, I cannot see.'

So death it was he knew behind that sheet
Of skin; darkness behind its passive light.
And all around him, while he spoke, there beat
    The endless drummers of subtracting night.

JOHN SHORT

CAROL

There was a Boy bedded in bracken
    Like to a sleeping snake all curled he lay
        On his thin navel turned this spinning sphere
            Each feeble finger fetched seven suns away
                He was not dropped in good-for-lambing weather
                He took no suck when shook buds sing together
                But he is come in cold-as-workhouse weather
                  Poor as a Salford child.

C. H. SISSON

THE NATURE OF MAN

It is the nature of man that puzzles me
As I walk from Saint James's Square to Charing Cross;
The polite mechanicals are going home,
I understand their condition and their loss.

Ape-like in that their box of wires
Is shut behind a face of human resemblance,
They favour a comic hat between their ears
And their monkey's tube is tucked inside their pants.

Language which is all our lies has us on a skewer,
Inept, weak, the grinning devil of comprehension; but sleep
Knows us for plants or undiscovered worlds;
If we have reasons, they lie deep.

IGHTHAM WOODS

The few syllables of a horse's scuffle at the edge of the road
Reach me in the green light of the beeches
Les seuls vrais plaisirs
Selon moy
Are those of one patch between the feet and the throat.
Possibly, but the beeches
And that half clop on the gravel
Indicate a world into which I can dissolve.

ADAM AND EVE

They must be shown as about to taste of the tree.
If they had already done so they would be like us;
If they were not about to do so they would be
Not our first parents but monsters.

You must show that they were the first who contrived
An act which has since become common,
With head held high when it is conceived
And, when it is repented of, dangling.

There must be not one Adam but two,
The second nailed upon the tree:
He came down in order to go up
Although he hangs so limply.

The first Adam, you will recall, gave birth
To a woman out of his side;
For the second the process was reversed
And that one was without pride.

CRANMER

Cranmer was parson of this parish
And said Our Father beside barns
Where my grandfather worked without praying.

From the valley came the ring of metal
And the horses clopped down the track by the stream
As my mother saw them.

The Wiltshire voices floated up to him.
How should they not overcome his proud Latin
With We depart answering his *Nunc Dimittis*?

One evening he came over the hillock   C. H.
To the edge of the church-yard already filled with SISSON
    bones
And saw in the smithy his own fire burning.

DARK SONG

The fire was furry as a bear
And the flames purr...
The brown bear rambles in his chain
Captive to cruel men
Through the dark and hairy wood.
The maid sighed, 'All my blood
Is animal. They thought I sat
Like a household cat;
But through the dark woods rambled I...
Oh, if my blood would die!'
The fire had a bear's fur;
It heard and knew...
The dark earth furry as a bear,
Grumbled too!

THE DRUM

(*The Narrative of the Demon of Tedworth*)

In his tall senatorial,
Black and manorial,
House where decoy-duck
Dust doth clack—
Clatter and quack
To a shadow black,—
Said the musty Justice Mompesson,
'What is that dark stark beating drum
That we hear rolling like the sea?'
'It is a beggar with a pass
Signed by you.' 'I signed not one.'

EDITH
SITWELL

They took the ragged drum that we
Once heard rolling like the sea;
In the house of the Justice it must lie
And usher in Eternity.

. . . .

Is it black night?
Black as Hecate howls a star
Wolfishly, and whined
The wind from very far.

In the pomp of the Mompesson house is one
Candle that lolls like the midnight sun,
Or the coral comb of a cock; . . . it rocks . . .
Only the goatish snow's locks
Watch the candles lit by fright
One by one through the black night.

Through the kitchen there runs a hare—
Whinnying, whines like grass, the air;
It passes; now is standing there
A lovely lady . . . see her eyes—
Black angels in a heavenly place,
Her shady locks and her dangerous grace.

'I thought I saw the wicked old witch in
The richest gallipot in the kitchen!'
A lolloping galloping candle confesses.
'Outside in the passage are wildernesses
Of darkness rustling like witches' dresses.'

Out go the candles one by one
Hearing the rolling of a drum!

What is the march we hear groan
As the hoofed sound of a drum marched on

EDITH SITWELL

With a pang like darkness, with a clang
Blacker than an orang-outang?
'Heliogabalus is alone,—
Only his bones to play upon!'

The mocking money in the pockets
Then turned black . . . now caws
The fire . . . outside, one scratched the door
As with iron claws,—

Scratching under the children's bed
And up the trembling stairs . . . 'Long dead'
Moaned the water black as crape.
Over the snow the wintry moon
Limp as henbane, or herb paris,
Spotted the bare trees; and soon
Whinnying, neighed the maned blue wind
Turning the burning milk to snow,
Whining it shied down the corridor—
Over the floor I heard it go
Where the drum rolls up the stair, nor tarries.

HEART AND MIND

Said the Lion to the Lioness—'When you are amber
    dust,—
No more a raging fire like the heat of the Sun
(No liking but all lust)—
Remember still the flowering of the amber blood and
    bone

The rippling of bright muscles like a sea
Remember the rose-prickles of bright paws
Though we shall mate no more
Till the fire of that sun the heart and the moon-cold
    bone are one.'

EDITH SITWELL

Said the Skeleton lying upon the sands of Time—
'The great gold planet that is the mourning heat of
    the Sun
Is greater than all gold, more powerful
Than the tawny body of a Lion that fire consumes
Like all that grows or leaps . . . so is the heart
More powerful than all dust. Once I was Hercules
Or Samson, strong as the pillars of the seas:
But the flames of the heart consumed me, and the
    mind
Is but a foolish wind.'

Said the Sun to the Moon—'When you are but a
    lonely white crone,
And I, a dead King in my golden armour somewhere
    in a dark wood,
Remember only this of our hopeless love
That never till Time is done
Will the fire of the heart and the fire of the mind be
    one.'

THE COAT OF FIRE

Amid the thunders of the falling Dark
In Tartarean darkness of the fog
I walk, a Pillar of Fire
On pavements of black marble, hard
And wide as the long boulevard
Of Hell . . . I, in whose veins the Furies wave
Their long fires, move where purgatories, heavens,
    hells and worlds
Wrought by illusion, hide in the human breast
And tear the enclosing heart . . . And the snow fell
(Thin flakes of ash from Gomorrah) on blind faces
Turned to the heedless sky . . . A dress has the sound

EDITH
SITWELL
Of Reality, reverberates like thunder.
And ghosts of aeons and of equinoxes
(Of moments that seemed aeons, and long partings)
Take on the forms of fashionable women
With veils that hide a new Catastrophe, and under
Is the fall of a world that was a heart. Some doomed
    to descend
Through all the hells and change into the Dog
Without its faithfulness, the Crocodile
Without its watchfulness, and then to Pampean mud.
In the circles of the city's hells beneath the fog
These bear, to light them, in the human breast,
The yellow dull light from the raging human dust,
The dull blue light from the brutes, light red as rust
Of blood from eyeless weeping ghosts, light black as
    smoke
From hell. And those breasts bear
No other light.... They circle in the snow
Where in the dust the apterous
Fates turned insects whisper 'Now abandon
Man the annelida. Let all be wingless
That hangs between the abyss and Abaddon.'
The Catastrophes with veils and trains drift by,
And I to my heart, disastrous Comet, cry
'Red heart, my Lucifer, how fallen art thou,
And lightless, I!'
The dresses sweep the dust of mortality
And roll the burden of Atlas' woe, changed to a stone
Up to the benches where the beggars sway—
Their souls alone as on the Judgement Day—
In their Valley of the myriad Dry Bones under
    world-tall houses.
Then, with a noise as if in the thunders of the Dark
All sins, griefs, aberrations of the world rolled to
    confess,

Those myriad Dry Bones rose to testify:
'See her, the Pillar of Fire!
                        The aeons of Cold
And all the deaths that Adam has endured
Since the first death, can not outfreeze our night.
And where is the fire of love that will warm our
    hands?
There is only this conflagration
Of all the sins of the world! To the dust's busyness
She speaks of annihilation
Of every form of dust, burned down to Nothingness!
To the small lovers, of a kiss that seems the red
Lightning of Comets firing worlds—and of a Night
That shall outburn all nights that lovers know—
The last red Night before the Judgement Day!
O Pillar of Flame, that drifts across the world to
    Nowhere!
The eyes are seas of fire! All forms, all sights,
And all sensations are on fire! All smells, a ravening
Raging cyclone of wild fire! The nose, burned quite
    away!
The tongue is on fire, all tastes on fire, the mind
Is red as noon upon the Judgement Day!
The tears are rolling, falling worlds of fire!
With what are these on fire? With passion, hate,
Infatuation, and old age, and death,
With sorrow, longing, and with labouring breath,
And with despair and life are these on fire!
With the illusions of the world, the flames of lust,
And raging red desire!
A Pillar of Fire is she in the emptying dust,
And will not change those fires into warmth for our
    hands,'
Said the beggars, lolling and rocking
The heedless world upon a heaving shoulder.

EDITH SITWELL

MOST LOVELY SHADE

EDITH SITWELL

Most lovely Dark, my Aethiopia born
Of the shade's richest splendour, leave not me
Where in the pomp and splendour of the shade
The dark air's leafy plumes no more a lulling music
    made.

Dark is your fleece, and dark the airs that grew
Amid those weeping leaves.
Plantations of the East drop precious dew
That, ripened by the light, rich leaves perspire.
Such are the drops that from the dark airs' feathers
    flew.

Most lovely Shade ... Syrinx and Dryope
And that smooth nymph that changed into a tree
Are dead ... the shade, that Aethiopia, sees
Their beauty make more bright its treasuries—
Their amber blood in porphyry veins still grows
Deep in the dark secret of the rose
And the smooth stem of many a weeping tree,
And in your beauty grows.

Come then, my pomp and splendour of the shade
Most lovely cloud that the hot sun made black
As dark-leaved airs,—
                  Come then, O precious cloud,
Lean to my heart: no shade of a rich tree
Shall pour such splendour as your heart to me.

THE YOUTH WITH RED-GOLD HAIR   Edith Sitwell

The gold-armoured ghost from the Roman road
Sighed over the wheat
'Fear not the sound and the glamour
Of my gold armour—
(The sound of the wind and the wheat)
Fear not its clamour. . . .
Fear only the red-gold sun with the fleece of a fox
Who will steal the fluttering bird you hide in your
    breast.
Fear only the red-gold rain
That will dim your brightness, O my tall tower of the
    corn,
You,—my blonde girl. . . .'
But the wind sighed, 'Rest.' . . .
The wind in his grey knight's armour
The wind in his grey night armour
Sighed over the fields of wheat, 'He is gone . . .
    Forlorn.'

STEVIE SMITH

THE LITTLE BOY LOST

The wood was rather old and dark
The witch was very ugly
And if it hadn't been for father
Walking there so smugly
I never should have followed
The beckoning of her finger.
Ah me how long ago it was
And still I linger
Under the ever interlacing beeches
Over a carpet of moss
I lift my hand but it never reaches
To where the breezes toss
The sun-kissed leaves above.
The sun?
Beware.
The sun never comes here.
Round about and round I go
Up and down and to and fro
The woodlouse hops upon the tree
Or should do but I really cannot see.
Happy fellow. Why can't I be
Happy as he?
The wood grows darker every day
It's not a bad place in a way
But I lost the way
Last Tuesday
Did I love father, mother, home?
Not very much; but now they're gone
I think of them with kindly toleration
Bred inevitability of separation.

Really if I could find some food
I should be happy enough in this wood
But darker days and hungrier I must spend
Till hunger and darkness make an end.

THE BEREAVED SWAN

Wan
Swan
On the lake
Like a cake
Of soap
Why is the swan
Wan
On the lake?
He has abandoned hope.

Wan
Swan
On the lake afloat
Bows his head:
O would that I were dead
For her sake that lies
Wrapped from my eyes
In a mantle of death,
The swan saith.

THE RIVER GOD
Of the River Mimram in Hertfordshire.

I may be smelly and I may be old,
Rough in my pebbles, reedy in my pools,
But where my fish float by I bless their swimming
And I like the people to bathe in me, especially
    women.

STEVIE But I can drown the fools
SMITH Who bathe too close to the weir, contrary to rules.
And they take a long time drowning
As I throw them up now and then in a spirit of
  clowning.
Hi yih, yippity-yap, merrily I flow,
O I may be an old foul river but I have plenty of go.
Once there was a lady who was too bold
She bathed in me by the tall black cliff where the
  water runs cold,
So I brought her down here
To be my beautiful dear.
Oh will she stay with me will she stay
This beautiful lady, or will she go away?
She lies in my beautiful deep river bed with many a
  weed
To hold her, and many a waving reed.
Oh who would guess what a beautiful white face lies
  there
Waiting for me to smooth and wash away the fear
She looks at me with. Hi yih, do not let her
Go. There is no one on earth who does not forget
  her
Now. They say I am a foolish old smelly river
But they do not know of my wide original bed
Where the lady waits, with her golden sleepy head.
If she wishes to go I will not forgive her.

THE WEAK MONK

The monk sat in his den,
He took the mighty pen
And wrote 'Of God and Men'.

One day the thought struck him
It was not according to Catholic doctrine;
His blood ran dim.

He wrote till he was ninety years old,
Then he shut the book with a clasp of gold
And buried it under the sheep fold.

He'd enjoyed it so much, he loved to plod,
And he thought he'd a right to expect that God
Would rescue his book alive from the sod.

Of course it rotted in the snow and rain;
No one will ever know now what he wrote of God
    and men.
For this the monk is to blame.

TO THE TUNE OF THE COVENTRY CAROL

The nearly right
And yet not quite
In love is wholly evil
And every heart
That loves in part
Is mortgaged to the devil.

I loved or thought
I loved in sort
Was this to love akin
To take the best
And leave the rest
And let the devil in?

O lovers true
And others too
Whose best is only better
Take my advice
Shun compromise
Forget him and forget her.

THE HEAVENLY CITY

I sigh for the heavenly country,
Where the heavenly people pass,
And the sea is as quiet as a mirror
Of beautiful, beautiful glass.

I walk in the heavenly field,
With lilies and poppies bright,
I am dressed in a heavenly coat
Of polished white.

When I walk in the heavenly parkland
My feet on the pastures are bare,
Tall waves the grass, but no harmful
Creature is there.

At night I fly over the housetops,
And stand on the bright moony beams;
Gold are all heaven's rivers,
And silver her streams.

SYDNEY GOODSIR SMITH

THE DEEVIL'S WALTZ

Rin and rout, rin and rout,
Mahoun gars us birl about,
He skirls his pipes, he stamps his heel,
The globe spins wud in a haliket reel.

There, the statesman's silken cheats,
Here, the bairnless mither greits;
There, a tyrant turns the screw,
Here, twa luvers' broken vous.

Enemies out, enemies in,
Truth a hure wi the pox gane blind;
Nou luvers' lips deny luve's name
And get for breid a chuckie-stane.

We kenna hert, we kenna heid,
The deil has thirlit quick and deid;
Jehovah snores and Christ his-sel
Lowps in the airms o Jezebel.

The sweit that rins frae his thornit brou
Is black as the standan teats o his cou;
I' the waltz o tears, and daith, and lees,
Juliet's fyled wi harlotries.

Och, luve itself at Hornie's lauch
Skeers like a caunel i the draucht;
The dance is on, the waltz o hell,
The wind frae its fleean skirts is snell.

SYDNEY GOODSIR SMITH

It whips black storm frae lochan's calm,
Sets banshees in the house o dwaum,
Gars black bluid spate the hert o me
—And waters guid sirs' barley-bree!

A wheen damned feckless fanatics
Wad halt the borneheid dance o Styx
—Their cry o truth the whirlwind reaps,
For pitie's deid and mercie sleeps.

Orpheus alane dow sauve frae deid
His ravisht Bride gin but she'd heed—
Ay, luve and richt like Albyn's life
Hing wi a threid, kisst by a knife.

Nichtlie, owre the huddert toun
The pipes and fiddles screich and boom,
The chaudron's steered by Maestro Nick
Wi a sanct's hoch-bane for parritch-stick

He lauchs his lauch, the angels greit
Wi joy as they dine on carrion meat;
Ablow, bumbazed dumbfoundert cods,
We seek the sternes in dubs and bogs.

Our ingyne's deaved, our mous are shut,
Our saul contract like a runkelt nut,
Een canna see the treen for the wuid
And hert's gane dreich for want o bluid.

For want o luve we live on hate,
For want o hevin praise the State,
For want o richts we worship rules,
For want o gods the glibbest fules.

Obey, obey! Ye maunna spier!
Liberties's forjeskit lear!
While Cloutie pipes it's crime to think
—It's taxed e'en hiecher nor the drink!

Och, rin and rout, we birl about
Til the rhythm o the Deil's jack-boot,
Black as auld widdie-fruit, Mahoun
Bestrides a redeless mapamound.

Halloween 1943

BOAT POEM

I wish there were a touch of these boats about my life;
so to speak, a tarring,
the touch of inspired disorder and something more
 than that,
something more too
than the mobility of sails or a primitive bumpy engine,
under that tiny hot-house window,
which eats up oil and benzine perhaps
but will go on beating in spite of the many strains
not needing with luck to be repaired too often,
with luck lasting years piled on years.

There must be a kind of envy which brings me peering
and nosing at the boats along the island quay
either in the hot morning
with the lace-light shaking up against their hulls from
 the water
or when their mast-tops
keep on drawing lines between stars.
(I do not speak here of the private yachts from the
clubs which stalk across the harbour like magnificent
white cats but sheer off and keep mostly to themselves.)

Look for example at the Bartolome; a deck-full
of mineral water and bottles of beer in cases
and great booming barrels of wine from the mainland,
endearing trade;
and lengths of timber and iron rods for building
and, curiously, a pig with flying ears
ramming a wet snout into whatever it explores.

Or the Virgen del Pilar, mantled and weavy with
    drooping nets
PM/708/3A
with starfish and pieces of cod drying on the wheel-
    house roof
some wine, the remains of supper on an enamel plate
and trousers and singlets 'passim';
both of these boats stinky and forgivable like some
    great men
both needing paint,
but both, one observes, armoured far better than us
    against jolts
by a belt of old motor-tyres lobbed round their sides
    for buffers.

And having in their swerving planks and in the point
    of their bows
the never-enough-to-be-praised
authority of a great tradition, the sea-shape
simple and true like a vase,
something that stays too in the carved head of an eagle
or that white-eyed wooden hound crying up beneath
    the bowsprit.

Qualities clearly admirable. So is their response to the
    occasion,
how they celebrate such times
and suddenly fountain with bunting and stand like
    ocean maypoles
on a Saints Day when a gun bangs from the fortifica-
    tions,
and an echo-gun throws a bang back
and all the old kitchen bells start hammering from the
    churches.

BERNARD Admirable again
SPENCER how one of them, perhaps tomorrow, will have gone
        with no hooting or fuss,
    simply absent from its place among the others,
    occupied, without self-importance, in the thousands-
        of-millions-of sea.

STEPHEN SPENDER

MARSTON

Marston, dropping it in the grate, broke his pipe.
Nothing hung on this act, it was no symbol
Ludicrous for calamity, but merely ludicrous.

That heavy-wrought briar with the great pine face
Now split across like a boxer's hanging dream
Of punishing a nigger, he brought from the
    continent;
It was his absurd relic, like bones,
Of stamping on the white-faced mountains,
Early beds in huts, and other journeys.

To hold the bank of the Danube, the slow barges
    down the river,
Those coracles with faces painted on,
Demanded his last money,
A foodless journey home, as pilgrimage.

'YOUR BODY IS STARS'

Your body is stars whose million glitter here:
I am lost amongst the branches of this sky
Here near my breast, here in my nostrils, here
Where our vast arms like streams of fire lie.

How can this end? My healing fills the night
And hangs its flags in worlds I cannot hear.
Our movements range through miles, and when we
    kiss
The moment widens to enclose long years.

* * *

STEPHEN Beholders of the promised dawn of truth
SPENDER The explorers of immense and simple lines,
Here is our goal, men cried, but it was lost
Amongst the mountain mists and mountain pines.

So with this face of love, whose breathings are
A mystery shadowed on the desert floor:
The promise hangs, this swarm of stars and flowers,
And then there comes the shutting of a door.

SONG

Stranger, you who hide my love
   In the curved cheek of a smile
And sleep with her upon a tongue
   Of soft lies which beguile,
     Your paradisal ecstasy
     Is justified is justified
By hunger of all beasts beneath
   The overhanging cloud,
     Who, to snatch quick pleasure run,
     Before their momentary sun
Be eclipsed by death.

Lightly, lightly from my sleep
   She stole, our vows of dew to break,
Upon a day of melting rain
   Another love to take;
     Her happy happy perfidy
     Was justified was justified
Since compulsive needs of sense
   Clamour to be satisfied
     And she was never one to miss
     The plausible happiness
Of a new experience.

STEPHEN SPENDER

I, who stand beneath a bitter
   Blasted tree, with the green life
Of summer joy cut from my side
   By that self-justifying knife,
     In my exiled misery
Were justified were justified
If upon two lives I preyed
   Or punished with my suicide,
     Or murdered pity in my heart
     Or two other lives did part
To make the world pay what I paid.

Oh, supposing that I climb
   Alone to a high room of clouds
Up a ladder of the time
And lie upon a bed alone
   And tear a feather from a wing
And listen to the world below
And write round my high paper walls
   Anything and everything
Which I know and do not know!

J. C. SQUIRE

UNDER

In this house, she said, in this high second storey,
In this room where we sit, over the midnight street,
There runs a rivulet, narrow but very rapid,
Under the still floor and your unconscious feet.

The lamp on the table made a cone of light
That spread to the base of the walls: above was in gloom.
I heard her words with surprise; had I worked here so long,
And never divined the secret of the room?

'But how,' I asked, 'does the water climb so high?'
'I do not know,' she said, 'but the thing is there;
Pull up the boards while I go and fetch you a rod.'
She passed, and I heard her creaking descend the stair.

And I rose and rolled the Turkey carpet back
From the two broad boards by the north wall she had named,
And, hearing already the crumple of water, I knelt
And lifted the first of them up; and the water gleamed,

Bordered with little frosted heaps of ice,
And, as she came back with a rod and line that swung,
I moved the other board; in the yellow light
The water trickled frostily, slackly along.

I took the tackle, a stiff black rubber worm,   J. C.
That stuck out its pointed tail from a cumbrous hook. Squire
'But there can't be fishing in water like this,' I said,
And she, with weariness, 'There is no ice there.
    Look.'

And I stood there, gazing down at a stream in spate,
Holding the rod in my undecided hand . . .
Till it all in a moment grew smooth and still and
    clear,
And along its deep bottom of slaty grey sand

Three scattered little trout, as black as tadpoles,
Came waggling slowly along the glass-dark lake,
And I swung my arm to drop my pointing worm in,
And then I stopped again with a little shake.

For I heard the thin gnat-like voices of the trout
—My body felt woolly and sick and astray and cold—
Crying with mockery in them: 'You are not allowed
To take us, you know, under ten years old.'

And the room swam, the calm woman and the yellow
    lamp,
The table, and the dim-glistering walls, and the floor
And the stream sank away, and all whirled dizzily,
And I moaned, and the pain at my heart grew more
    and more,

And I fainted away, utterly miserable,
Falling in a place where there was nothing to pass,
Knowing all sorrows and the mothers and sisters of
    sorrows,
And the pain of the darkness before anything ever
    was.

THE ABSINTHE-DRINKER

Gently I wave the visible world away.
Far off, I hear a roar, afar yet near,
Far off and strange, a voice is in my ear,
And is the voice my own? the words I say
Fall strangely, like a dream, across the day;
And the dim sunshine is a dream. How clear,
New as the world to lovers' eyes, appear
The men and women passing on their way!

The world is very fair. The hours are all
Linked in a dance of mere forgetfulness.
I am at peace with God and man. O glide,
Sands of the hour-glass that I count not, fall
Serenely: scarce I feel your soft caress,
Rocked on this dreamy and indifferent tide.

NERVES

The modern malady of love is nerves.
Love, once a simple madness, now observes
The stages of his passionate disease,
And is twice sorrowful because he sees,
Inch by inch entering, the fatal knife.
O health of simple minds, give me your life,
And let me, for one midnight, cease to hear
The clock for ever ticking in my ear,
The clock that tells the minutes in my brain.
It is not love, nor love's despair, this pain

That shoots a witless, keener pang across
The simple agony of love and loss.
Nerves, Nerves! O folly of a child who dreams
Of heaven, and, waking in the darkness, screams.

ARTHUR SYMONS

THE GREY WOLF

The grey wolf comes again: I had made fast
The door with chains; how has the grey wolf passed
My threshold? I have nothing left to give;
Go from me now, grey wolf, and let me live!
I have fed you once, given all you would, given all
I had to give. I have been prodigal;
I am poor now, the table is but spread
With water and a little wheaten bread;
You have taken all I ever had from me:
Go from me now, grey wolf, and let me be!

The grey wolf, crouching by the bolted door,
Waits, watching for his food upon the floor;
I see the old hunger and the old thirst of blood
Rise up, under his eyelids, like a flood;
What shall I do that the grey wolf may go?
This time, I have no store of meat to throw;
He waits; but I have nothing, and I stand
Helpless, and his eyes fasten on my hand.
O grey wolf, grey wolf, will you not depart,
This time, unless I feed you with my heart?

DYLAN THOMAS

'BEFORE I KNOCKED AND FLESH LET ENTER'

Before I knocked and flesh let enter,
With liquid hands tapped on the womb,
I who was shapeless as the water
That shaped the Jordan near my home
Was brother to Mnetha's daughter
And sister to the fathering worm.

I who was deaf to spring and summer,
Who knew not sun nor moon by name,
Felt thud beneath my flesh's armour,
As yet was in a molten form,
The leaden stars, the rainy hammer
Swung by my father from his dome.

I knew the message of the winter,
And darted hail, the childish snow,
And the wind was my sister suitor;
Wind in me leaped, the hellborn dew;
My veins flowed with the Eastern weather;
Ungotten I knew night and day.

As yet ungotten, I did suffer;
The rack of dreams my lily bones
Did twist into a living cipher,
And flesh was snipped to cross the lines
Of gallow crosses on the liver
And brambles in the wringing brains.

My throat knew thirst before the structure
Of skin and vein around the well
Where words and water make a mixture
Unfailing till the blood runs foul;
My heart knew love, my belly hunger;
I smelt the maggot in my stool.

And time cast forth my mortal creature
To drift or drown upon the seas
Acquainted with the salt adventure
Of tides that never touch the shores.
I who was rich was made the richer
By sipping at the vine of days.

I, born of flesh and ghost, was neither
A ghost nor man, but mortal ghost.
And I was struck down by death's feather.
I was a mortal to the last
Long breath that carried to my father
The message of his dying christ.

You who bow down at cross and altar,
Remember me and pity Him
Who took my flesh and bone for armour
And doublecrossed my mother's womb.

THE HUNCHBACK IN THE PARK

The hunchback in the park
A solitary mister
Propped between trees and water
From the opening of the garden lock
That lets the trees and water enter
Until the Sunday sombre bell at dark

DYLAN
THOMAS
Eating bread from a newspaper
Drinking water from the chained cup
That the children filled with gravel
In the fountain basin where I sailed my ship
Slept at night in a dog kennel
But nobody chained him up.

Like the park birds he came early
Like the water he sat down
And Mister they called Hey mister
The truant boys from the town
Running when he had heard them clearly
On out of sound

Past lake and rockery
Laughing when he shook his paper
Hunchbacked in mockery
Through the loud zoo of the willow groves
Dodging the park keeper
With his stick that picked up leaves.

And the old dog sleeper
Alone between nurses and swans
While the boys among willows
Made the tigers jump out of their eyes
To roar on the rockery stones
And the groves were blue with sailors

Made all day until bell time
A woman figure without fault
Straight as a young elm
Straight and tall from his crooked bones
That she might stand in the night
After the locks and chains

All night in the unmade park
After the railings and shrubberies
The birds the grass the trees the lake
And the wild boys innocent as strawberries
Had followed the hunchback
To his kennel in the dark.

'THIS BREAD I BREAK WAS ONCE THE OAT'

This bread I break was once the oat,
This wine upon a foreign tree
Plunged in its fruit;
Man in the day or wind at night
Laid the crops low, broke the grape's joy.

Once in this wind the summer blood
Knocked in the flesh that decked the vine,
Once in this bread
The oat was merry in the wind;
Man broke the sun, pulled the wind down,

This flesh you break, this blood you let
Make desolation in the vein,
Were oat and grape
Born of the sensual root and sap;
My wine you drink, my bread you snap.

'EARS IN THE TURRETS HEAR'

Ears in the turrets hear
Hands grumble on the door,
Eyes in the gables see
The fingers at the locks.

DYLAN THOMAS

Shall I unbolt or stay
Alone till the day I die
Unseen by stranger-eyes
In this white house?
Hands, hold you poison or grapes?

Beyond this island bound
By a thin sea of flesh
And a bone coast,
The land lies out of sound
And the hills out of mind.
No bird or flying fish
Disturbs this island's rest.

Ears in this island hear
The wind pass like a fire,
Eyes in this island see
Ships anchor off the bay.
Shall I run to the ships
With the wind in my hair,
Or stay till the day I die
And welcome no sailor?
Ships, hold you poison or grapes?

Hands grumble on the door,
Ships anchor off the bay,
Rain beats the sand and slates.
Shall I let in the stranger,
Shall I welcome the sailor,
Or stay till the day I die?

Hands of the stranger and holds of the ships,
Hold you poison or grapes?

EDWARD THOMAS

THE CLOUDS THAT ARE SO LIGHT

As the clouds that are so light,
Beautiful, swift, and bright,
Cast shadows on field and park
Of the earth that is so dark,

And even so now, light one!
Beautiful, swift and bright one!
You let fall on a heart that was dark,
Unillumined, a deeper mark.

But clouds would have, without earth
To shadow, far less worth:
Away from your shadow on me
Your beauty less would be,

And if it still be treasured
An age hence, it shall be measured
By this small dark spot
Without which it were not.

TALL NETTLES

Tall nettles cover up, as they have done
These many springs, the rusty harrow, the plough
Long worn out, and the roller made of stone:
Only the elm butt tops the nettles now.

This corner of the farmyard I like most:
As well as any bloom upon a flower
I like the dust on the nettles, never lost
Except to prove the sweetness of a shower.

EDWARD THOMAS

THE SUN USED TO SHINE

The sun used to shine while we two walked
Slowly together, paused and started
Again, and sometimes mused, sometimes talked
As either pleased, and cheerfully parted

Each night. We never disagreed
Which gate to rest on. The to be
And the late past we gave small heed.
We turned from men or poetry

To rumours of the war remote
Only till both stood disinclined
For aught but the yellow flavorous coat
Of an apple wasps had undermined;

Or a sentry of dark betonies,
The stateliest of small flowers on earth,
At the forest verge; or crocuses
Pale purple as if they had their birth

In sunless Hades fields. The war
Came back to mind with the moonrise
Which soldiers in the east afar
Beheld then. Nevertheless, our eyes

Could as well imagine the Crusades
Or Caesar's battles. Everything
To faintness like those rumours fades—
Like the brook's water glittering

Under the moonlight—like those walks
Now—like us two that took them, and
The fallen apples, all the talks
The silences—like memory's sand

When the tide covers it late or soon,
And other men through other flowers
In those fields under the same moon
Go talking and have easy hours.

THE OWL

Downhill I came, hungry, and yet not starved;
Cold, yet had heat within me that was proof
Against the North wind; tired, yet so that rest
Had seemed the sweetest thing under a roof.

Then at the inn I had food, fire, and rest,
Knowing how hungry, cold, and tired was I.
All of the night was quite barred out except
An owl's cry, a most melancholy cry

Shaken out long and clear upon the hill,
No merry note, nor cause of merriment,
But one telling me plain what I escaped
And others could not, that night, as in I went.

And salted was my food, and my repose,
Salted and sobered, too, by the bird's voice
Speaking for all who lay under the stars,
Soldiers and poor, unable to rejoice.

SNOW

In the gloom of whiteness,
In the great silence of snow,
A child was sighing
And bitterly saying: 'Oh,

EDWARD They have killed a white bird up there on her nest,
THOMAS The down is fluttering from her breast!'
   And still it fell through that dusky brightness
   On the child crying for the bird of the snow.

THAW

   Over the land freckled with snow half-thawed
   The speculating rooks at their nests cawed
   And saw from elm-tops, delicate as flower of grass,
   What we below could not see, Winter pass.

R. S. THOMAS

THE SURVIVOR

Yesterday I found one left:
Eighty-five, too old for mischief.
What strange grace lends him a brief
Time for repenting of his theft
Of health and comeliness from her
Who lay caught in his strong arms
Night by night and heard the farm's
Noises, the beasts' moan and stir?

The land's thug: seventeen stone,
Settling down in a warm corner
By a wood fire's lazy purr;
A slumped bundle of fat and bone,
Bragging endlessly of his feats
Of strength and skill with the long scythe,
Or gallantry among the blithe
Serving women, all on heat

For him, of course. My mind went back
Sombrely to that rough parish,
Lovely as the eye could wish
In its green clothes, but beaten black
And blue by the deeds of dour men
Too like him, warped inside
And given to watching, sullen-eyed,
Love still-born, as it was then.

Wake him up. It is too late
Now for the blood's foolish dreaming.
The veins clog and the body's spring
Is long past; pride and hate

R. S. Thomas

Are the strong's fodder and the young.
Old and weak, he must chew now
The cud of prayer and be taught how
From hard hearts huge tears are wrung.

TERENCE TILLER

READING A MEDAL

who, minter of medallions,
casting or striking, caused me so
to speak with double voice in bronze,
I may not help and cannot know.
But I am Pallas, and I bear
the mask of war by wisdom; you
shall spin my olives to despair:
all my reverse will say is true.

>   (*Turn me, and read that other side;
>   you must return: for, mask and coin,
>   I give no rest unless you ride
>   the felloe where my faces join*).

My face is Aphrodite's—she
that rules by myrtle and by dove;
I loose my zone to let you see
the end of reasoning by love.
Nothing my obverse tells is true:
turn till you read me as it was;
turn till you know me, and renew
my helpless paradox—because

CHARLES TOMLINSON

THE CHESTNUT AVENUE
AT ALTON HOUSE

Beneath their flames, cities of candelabra
    Gathering in a more than civic dark
Sway between green and gloom,
    Prepare a way of hushed submergence
Where the eye descries no human house,
    But a green trajectory whose depths
Glimmers a barrier of stone. At the wind's invasion
    The greenness teeters till the indented parallels
Lunge to a restive halt, defying still
    The patient geometry that planted them
Thus, in their swaying stations. We have lent them
    Order—they, greeting that gift
    With these incalculable returns. Mindless
    They lead the mind its ways, deny
The imposition of its frontiers, as the wind, their ally,
    Assails the civility of the facade they hide
Their green indifference barbarous at its panes.

W. J. TURNER

LIFE AND DEATH

I saw a vulture in the sky
Shadow of the desert sun
And lying white upon the sand
A bleached and perfect skeleton.

'Which is life and which is death?'
Came that instant to my mind.
Methought voluptuous where they lay
The bones to desert were calcined.

The desert panting in the sun,
Curled delight into a sigh;
Airless, burning for its breath
Gaped the blue and stainless sky.

Palpitating flew away
A Shadow smaller than a hand,
It was he who flew that lay
Stretched upon the desert sand.

AS LAMBS INTO THE PEN

As lambs into the pen of sheep
As dreams to some immortal sleep,
As stars into the starry fold
By the shepherd of the Heaven
Are herded in;
So to her pearly halls beneath
When the wind of light is cold
Moon goes misty to her death
With Endymion as of old;

Love to Death is gathered in.

Faint upon the lake at dawn
Lies a star as star on glass,
So my languor lies on thine:
Faint as fire with sun upon it,
Gold to silver beaten thin,
Dying of its own delight:

Love to Death is gathered in.

VERNON WATKINS

THE FEATHER

I stoop to gather a seabird's feather
Fallen on the beach,
Torn from a beautiful drifting wing;
What can I learn or teach,
Running my finger through the comb
And along the horny quill?
The body it was torn from
Gave out a cry so shrill,
Sailors looked from their white road
To see what help was there.
It dragged the winds to a drop of blood
Falling through drowned air,
Dropping from the sea-hawk's beak,
From frenzied talons sharp;
Now if the words they lost I speak
It must be to that harp
Under the strange, light-headed sea
That bears a straw of the nest.
Unless I make that melody,
How can the dead have rest?

Sheer from wide air to the wilderness
The victim fell, and lay;
The starlike bone is fathomless,
Lost among wind and spray.
This lonely, isolated thing
Trembles amid their sound.
I set my finger on the string
That spins the ages round.
But let it sleep, let it sleep

VERNON WATKINS

Where shell and stone are cast;
Its ecstasy the Furies keep,
For nothing here is past.
The perfect into night must fly;
On this the winds agree.
How could a blind rock satisfy
The hungers of the sea?

INDOLENCE

Count up those books whose pages you have read
Moulded by water. Wasps this paper made.
Come. You have taken tribute from the dead.
Your tribute to the quick must now be paid.

What lovelier tribute than to rest your head
Beneath this birchtree which is bound to fade?
And watch the branches quivering by a thread
Beyond interpretation of the shade.

THE COLLIER

When I was born on Amman hill
A dark bird crossed the sun.
Sharp on the floor the shadow fell,
I was the youngest son.

And when I went to the County School
I worked in a shaft of light.
In the wood of the desk I cut my name:
Dai for Dynamite.

VERNON
WATKINS

The tall black hills my brothers stood;
Their lessons all were done.
From the door of the school when I ran out
They frowned to watch me run.

The slow grey bells they rung a chime
Surly with grief or age.
Clever or clumsy, lad or lout,
All would look for a wage.

I learnt the valley flowers' names
And the rough bark knew my knees.
I brought home trout from the river
And spotted eggs from the trees.

A coloured coat I was given to wear
Where the lights of the rough land shone.
Still jealous of my favour
The tall black hills looked on.

They dipped my coat in the blood of a kid
And they cast me down a pit,
And although I crossed with strangers
There was no way up from it.

Soon as I went from the County School
I worked in a shaft. Said Jim,
'You will get your chain of gold, my lad,
But not for a likely time.'

And one said, 'Jack was not raised up
When the wind blew out the light
Though he interpreted their dreams
And guessed their fears by night.'

VERNON
WATKINS

And Tom, he shivered his leper's lamp
For the stain that round him grew;
And I heard mouths pray in the after-damp
When the picks would not break through.

They changed words there in the darkness
And still through my head they run,
And white on my limbs is the linen sheet
And gold on my neck the sun.

THE HEALING OF THE LEPER

O, have you seen the leper healed,
And fixed your eyes upon his look?
There is the book of God revealed.
And God has made no other book.

The withered hand which time interred
Grasps in a moment the unseen.
The word we had not heard, is heard:
What we are then, we had not been.

Plotinus, preaching on heaven's floor,
Could not give praise like that loud cry
Bursting the bondage of death's door;
For we die once; indeed we die.

What Sandro Botticelli found
Rose from the river where we bathe:
Music the air, the stream, the ground;
Music the dove, the rock, the faith:

And all that music whirled upon
The eyes' deep-sighted, burning rays,

          Where all the prayers of labours done   VERNON
          Are resurrected into praise.   WATKINS

          But look: his face is like a mask
          Surrounded by the beat of wings.
          Because he knows that ancient task
          His true transfiguration springs.

          All fires the prophets' words contained
          Fly to those eyes, transfixed above.
          Their awful precept has remained:
          'Be nothing first; and then, be love.'

SWEDENBORG'S SKULL

Note this survivor, bearing the mark of the violator,
Yet still a vessel of uninterrupted calm.
Its converse is ended. They beat on the door of his coffin,
But they could not shake or destroy that interior psalm
Intended for God alone, for his sole Creator.
For gold they broke into his tomb.

The mark of the pick is upon him, that rough intrusion
Upon the threshold and still place of his soul.
With courtesy he received them. They stopped, astonished,
Where the senses had vanished, to see the dignified skull
Discoursing alone, entertaining those guests of his vision
Whose wit made the axe-edge dull.

Here the brain flashed its fugitive lightning, its secret appraising,
Where marble, settled in utmost composure, appears.

VERNON **Here** the heirs of the heavens were disposed in
WATKINS symmetrical orders
And a flash of perception transfigured the darkness of
years.
The mark of a membrane is linked with those
traffickers grazing
Its province of princes and spheres.

Where the robbers looked, meditations disputed the
legacy
Of the dreaming mind, and the rungs of their common-
place crime
Gave way to swift places of angels, caught up in
division
From the man upon earth; but his patience now
played like a mime,
And they could not break down or interpret the skull
in its privacy
Or take him away from his time.

So I see it today, the inscrutable mask of conception
Arrested in death. Hard, slender and grey, it
transcends
The enquiring senses, even as a shell toiling inward,
Caught up from the waters of change by a traveller
who bends
His piercing scrutiny, yields but a surface deception,
Still guarding the peace it defends.

ANNA WICKHAM

THE EGOIST

Shall I write pretty poetry
Controlled by ordered sense in me
With an old choice of figure and of word,
So call my soul a nesting bird?
Of the dead poets I can make a synthesis,
And learn poetic form that in them is;
But I will use the figure that is real
For me, the figure that I feel.
And now of this matter of ear-perfect rhyme,
My clerk can list all language in his leisure time;
A faulty rhyme may be a well-placed microtone,
And hold a perfect imperfection of its own.

A poet rediscovers all creation;
His instinct gives him beauty, which is sensed
    relation.
It was as fit for one man's thought to trot in iambs, as
    it is for me,
Who live not in the horse-age, but in the day of
    aeroplanes, to write my rhythms free.

THE FIRED POT

In our town people live in rows.
The only irregular thing in a street is the steeple;
And where that points to, God only knows,
And not the poor disciplined people!
And I have watched the women growing old,
Passionate about pins, and pence, and soap,

ANNA Till the heart within my wedded breast grew cold,
WICK- And I lost hope.
  HAM But a young soldier came to our town,
       He spoke his mind most candidly.
       He asked me quickly to lie down,
       And that was very good for me.
       For though I gave him no embrace—
       Remembering my duty—
       He altered the expression of my face
       And gave me back my beauty.

MEDITATION AT KEW

Alas! for all the pretty women who marry dull men,
Go into the suburbs and never come out again,
Who lose their pretty faces, and dim their pretty eyes,
Because no one has skill or courage to organize.

What do these pretty women suffer when they
    marry?
They bear a boy who is like Uncle Harry,
A girl, who is like Aunt Eliza, and not new.
These old dull races must breed true.

I would enclose a common in the sun,
And let the young wives out to laugh and run;
I would steal their dull clothes and go away
And leave the pretty naked things to play.

Then I would make a contract with hard Fate
That they see all the men in the world to choose a
    mate,
And I would summon all the pipers in the town
That they dance with Love at a feast, and dance him
    down.

From the gay unions of choice
We'd have a race of splendid beauty, and of thrilling
    voice.
The World whips frank gay love with rods,
But frankly gaily shall we get the gods.

VANITY

I saw old Duchesses with their young loves,
I, in a pair of very shabby gloves,
Even my shapeless garments could not make me sad,
For I remembered I was young as you, dear lad,
That I am lovelier without my dress
Gave me sweet wanton happiness.

MOUNT BADON

The King's poet was his captain of horse in the wars.
He rode over the ridge; his force
sat hidden behind, as the king's mind had bidden.
The plain below held the Dragon in the centre,
Lancelot on the left, on the right Gawaine,
Bors in the rear commanding the small reserve:
the sea's indiscriminate host roared at the City's wall.
As with his household few Taliessin rode over the
 ridge,
the trumpets blew, the lines engaged.

Staring, motionless, he sat;
who of the pirates saw? none stopped;
they cropped and lopped Logres; they struck deep,
and their luck held; only support lacked:
neither for charge nor for ruse could the allied crews
abide the civilized single command;
each captain led his own band and each captain
 unbacked;
but numbers crashed; Taliessin saw Gawaine
fail, recover, and fail again;
he saw the Dragon sway; far away
the household of Lancelot was wholly lost in the fray;
he saw Bors fling
company after company to the aid of the king,
till the last waited the word alone.

Staring, motionless, he sat.
Dimly behind him he heard how his staff stirred.

One said: 'He dreams or makes verse'; one: 'Fool,
all lies in a passion of patience—my lord's rule.'
In a passion of patience he waited the expected
    second.
Suddenly the noise abated, the fight vanished, the last
few belated shouts died in a new quiet.
In the silence of a distance, clear to the king's poet's
    sight,
Virgil was standing on a trellised path by the sea.
Taliessin saw him negligently leaning; he felt
the deep breath dragging the depth of all dimension,
as the Roman sought for the word, sought for his
    thought,
sought for the invention of the City by the phrase.
He saw Virgil's unseeing eyes; his own,
in that passion of all activity but one suspended,
leaned on those screened ports of blind courage.
Barbaric centuries away, the ghostly battle contended.

Civilized centuries away, the Roman moved.
Taliessin saw the flash of his style
dash at the wax; he saw the hexameter spring,
and the king's sword swing; he saw, in the long field,
the point where the pirate chaos might suddenly
    yield,
the place for the law of grace to strike.
He stood in his stirrups; he stretched his hand;
he fetched the pen of his spear from its bearer;
his staff behind signed to their men.

The Æneid's beaked lines swooped on Actium;
the stooped horse charged; backward blown,
the flame of song streaked the spread spears
and the strung faces of words on a strong tongue.
The household of Taliessin swung on the battle;

CHARLES   hierarchs of freedom, golden candles of the solstice
WIL-   that flared round the golden-girdled Logos,
LIAMS   snowy-haired,
             brazen-footed, starry-handed, the thigh banded with
                the Name.

   The trumpets of the City blared through the feet of
      brass;
   the candles flared among the pirates; their mass broke;
   Bors flung his company forward; the horse and the
      reserve
   caught the sea's host in a double curve;
   the paps of the day were golden-girdled;
   hair, bleached white by the mere stress of the glory,
   drew the battle through the air up threads of light.
   The tor of Badon heard the analytical word;
   the grand art mastered the thudding hammer of Thor,
   and the heart of our lord Taliessin determined the
      war.

   The lord Taliessin kneeled to the king;
   the candles of new Camelot shone through the fought
      field.

TALIESSIN'S SONG OF THE UNICORN

Shouldering shapes of the skies of Broceliande
   are rumours in the flesh of Caucasia; they raid the
      west,
clattering with shining hooves, in myth scanned—
   centaur, gryphon, but lordlier for verse is the crest
of the unicorn, the quick panting unicorn; he will come
   to a girl's crooked finger or the sharp smell
of her clear flesh—but to her no good; the strum
   of her blood takes no riot or quiet from the quell;

she cannot like such a snorting alien love
   galloped from a dusky horizon it has no voice
to explain, nor the silver horn pirouetting above
   her bosom—a ghostly threat but no way to rejoice
in released satiation; her body without delight
   chill-curdled, and the gruesome horn only to be
polished, its rifling rubbed between breasts; right
     is the tale that a true man runs and sets the maid
        free,
and she lies with the gay hunter and his spear
        flesh-hued,
   and over their couch the spoiled head displayed—
as Lesbia tied horned Catullus—of the cuckold of the
        wood;
   such, west from Caucasia, is the will of every maid;
yet if any, having the cunning to call the grand beast,
   the animal which is but a shade till it starts to run,
should dare set palms on the point, twisting from the
        least
   to feel the sharper impress, for the thrust to stun
her arteries into channels of tears beyond blood
   (O twy-fount, crystal in crimson, of the Word's
        side),
and she to a background of dark bark, where the wood
   becomes one giant tree, were pinned, and plied
through hands to heart by the horn's longing: O she
   translucent, planted with virtues, lit by throes,
should be called the Mother of the Unicorn's Voice,
        men see
her with awe, her son the new sound that goes
surrounding the City's reach, the sound of enskied
   shouldering shapes, and there each science disposed,
horn-sharp, blood-deep, ocean and lightning wide,
   in her paramour's song, by intellectual nuptials
        unclosed.

LULLABY

Beloved, may your sleep be sound
That have found it where you fed.
What were all the world's alarms
To mighty Paris when he found
Sleep upon a golden bed
That first dawn in Helen's arms?

Sleep, beloved, such a sleep
As did that wild Tristram know
When, the potion's work being done,
Roe could run or doe could leap
Under oak and beechen bough,
Roe could leap or doe could run;

Such a sleep and sound as fell
Upon Eurotas' grassy bank
When the holy bird, that there
Accomplished his predestined will,
From the limbs of Leda sank
But not from her protecting care.

LONG-LEGGED FLY

That civilisation may not sink,
Its great battle lost,
Quiet the dog, tether the pony
To a distant post;
Our master Caesar is in the tent
Where the maps are spread,
His eyes fixed upon nothing,

A hand under his head.   W. B.
Like a long-legged fly upon the stream   YEATS
His mind moves upon silence.

That the topless towers be burnt
And men recall that face,
Move most gently if move you must
In this lonely place.
She thinks, part woman, three parts a child,
That nobody looks; her feet
Practise a tinker shuffle
Picked up on a street.
Like a long-legged fly upon the stream
Her mind moves upon silence.

That girls at puberty may find
The first Adam in their thought,
Shut the door of the Pope's chapel,
Keep those children out.
There on that scaffolding reclines
Michael Angelo.
With no more sound than the mice make
His hand moves to and fro.
Like a long-legged fly upon the stream
His mind moves upon silence.

PARTING

He. Dear, I must be gone
    While night shuts the eyes
    Of the household spies;
    That song announces dawn.

W. B. YEATS

She. No, night's bird and love's
    Bids all true lovers rest,
    While his loud song reproves
    The murderous stealth of day.

He. Daylight already flies
    From mountain crest to crest.

She. That light is from the moon.

He. That bird . . .

She.   Let him sing on,
    I offer to love's play
    My dark declivities.

THE LADY'S THIRD SONG
(From The Three Bushes*)*

When you and my true lover meet
And he plays tunes between your feet,
Speak no evil of the soul,
Nor think that body is the whole,
For I that am his daylight lady
Know worse evil of the body;
But in honour split his love
Till either neither have enough,
That I may hear if we should kiss
A contrapuntal serpent hiss,
You, should hand explore a thigh,
All the labouring heavens sigh.

THE CIRCUS ANIMALS' DESERTION

W. B. YEATS

I

I sought a theme and sought for it in vain,
I sought it daily for six weeks or so.
Maybe at last, being but a broken man,
I must be satisfied with my heart, although
Winter and summer till old age began
My circus animals were all on show,
Those stilted boys, that burnished chariot,
Lion and woman and the Lord knows what.

II

What can I but enumerate old themes?
First that sea-rider Oisin led by the nose
Through three enchanted islands, allegorical dreams,
Vain gaiety, vain battle, vain repose,
Themes of the embittered heart, or so it seems,
That might adorn old songs or courtly shows;
But what cared I that set him on to ride,
I starved for the bosom of his faery bride?

And then a counter-truth filled out its play,
The Countess Cathleen was the name I gave it;
She, pity-crazed, had given her soul away,
But masterful Heaven had intervened to save it
I thought my dear must her own soul destroy,
So did fanaticism and hate enslave it,
And this brought forth a dream and soon enough
This dream itself had all my thought and love.

And when the Fool and Blind Man stole the bread
Cuchulain fought the ungovernable sea;
Heart-mysteries there, and yet when all is said

W. B. It was the dream itself enchanted me:
YEATS Character isolated by a deed
To engross the present and dominate memory.
Players and painted stage took all my love,
And not those things that they were emblems of.

III

Those masterful images because complete
Grew in pure mind, but out of what began?
A mound of refuse or the sweepings of a street,
Old kettles, old bottles, and a broken can,
Old iron, old bones, old rags, that raving slut
Who keeps the till. Now that my ladder's gone,
I must lie down where all the ladders start,
In the foul rag-and-bone shop of the heart.

SONG FROM A PLAY

I saw a staring virgin stand
Where holy Dionysus died,
And tear the heart out of his side,
And lay the heart upon her hand
And bear that beating heart away;
And then did all the Muses sing
Of Magnus Annus at the spring,
As though God's death were but a play.

Another Troy must rise and set,
Another lineage feed the crow,
Another Argo's painted prow
Drive to a flashier bauble yet.
The Roman Empire stood appalled:
It dropped the reins of peace and war
When that fierce virgin and her Star
Out of the fabulous darkness called.

LAPIS LAZULI

(*For Harry Clifton*)

W. B. YEATS

I have heard that hysterical women say
They are sick of the palette and fiddle-bow,
Of poets that are always gay,
For everybody knows or else should know
That if nothing drastic is done
Aeroplane and Zeppelin will come out,
Pitch like King Billy bomb-balls in
Until the town lie beaten flat.

All perform their tragic play,
There struts Hamlet, there is Lear,
That's Ophelia, that Cordelia;
Yet they, should the last scene be there,
The great stage curtain about to drop,
If worthy their prominent part in the play,
Do not break up their lines to weep.
They know that Hamlet and Lear are gay;
Gaiety transfiguring all that dread.
All men have aimed at, found and lost;
Black out; Heaven blazing into the head:
Tragedy wrought to its uttermost.
Though Hamlet rambles and Lear rages,
And all the drop-scenes drop at once
Upon a hundred thousand stages,
It cannot grow by an inch or an ounce.

On their own feet they came, or on shipboard,
Camel-back, horse-back, ass-back, mule-back,
Old civilisations put to the sword.
Then they and their wisdom went to rack:
No handiwork of Callimachus,
Who handled marble as if it were bronze,

W. B. YEATS

Made draperies that seemed to rise
When sea-wind swept the corner, stands;
His long lamp-chimney shaped like the stem
Of a slender palm, stood but a day;
All things fall and are built again,
And those that build them again are gay.

Two Chinamen, behind them a third,
Are carved in lapis lazuli,
Over them flies a long-legged bird,
A symbol of longevity;
The third, doubtless a serving-man,
Carries a musical instrument.

Every discoloration of the stone,
Every accidental crack or dent,
Seems a water-course or an avalanche,
Or lofty slope where it still snows
Though doubtless plum or cherry-branch
Sweetens the little half-way house

Those Chinamen climb towards, and I
Delight to imagine them seated there;
There, on the mountain and the sky,
On all the tragic scene they stare.
One asks for mournful melodies;
Accomplished fingers begin to play.
Their eyes mid many wrinkles, their eyes,
Their ancient, glittering eyes, are gay.

ANDREW YOUNG

STAY, SPRING

Stay, spring, for by this ruthless haste
You turn all good to waste;
Look, how the blackthorn now
Changes to trifling dust upon the bough.

Where blossom from the wild pear shakes
Too rare a china breaks,
And though the cuckoos shout
They will forget their name ere June is out.

That thrush too, that with beadlike eye
Watches each passer-by,
Is warming at her breast
A brood that when they fly rob their own nest.

So late begun, so early ended!
Lest I should be offended
Take warning, spring, and stay
Or I might never turn to look your way.

THE SCARECROW

He strides across the grassy corn
That has not grown since it was born,
A piece of sacking on a pole,
A ghost, but nothing like a soul.

Why must this dead man haunt the spring
With arms anxiously beckoning?
Is spring not hard enough to bear
For one at autumn of his year?

ANDREW YOUNG

THE DEAD CRAB

A rosy shield upon its back,
That not the hardest storm could crack,
From whose sharp edge projected out
Black pin-point eyes staring about;
Beneath, the well-knit cote-armure
That gave to its weak belly power;
The clustered legs with plated joints
That ended in stiletto points;
The claws like mouths it held outside:—
I cannot think this creature died
By storm or fish or sea-fowl harmed
Walking the sea so heavily armed;
Or does it make for death to be
Oneself a living armoury?

THE BLACK ROCK OF KILTEARN

They named it Aultgraat—Ugly Burn,
This water through the crevice hurled
Scouring the entrails of the world—
Not ugly in the rising smoke
That clothes it with a rainbowed cloak
But slip a foot on frost-spiked stone
Above this rock-lipped Phlegethon
And you shall have
The Black Rock of Kiltearn
For tombstone, grave
And trumpet of your resurrection.

ACKNOWLEDGEMENTS

For permission to reprint copyright material, the following acknowledgements are made:

For poems by L. Aaronson, to the author.
Poems, 1933 (Gollancz).
Christ in the Synagogue (Gollancz).

For the poem by Lascelles Abercrombie, to his literary executors.
The Collected Poems of Lascelles Abercrombie (O.U.P.).

For the poem by Dannie Abse, to the author, Christy and Moore Ltd., and Hutchinson & Co. (Publishers) Ltd., London.
Walking Under Water (Hutchinson).

For poems by Drummond Allison, to his literary executors.
The Yellow Night (Fortune Press).

For poems by W. H. Auden, to the author and Faber & Faber Ltd.
For the Time Being (Faber).
Collected Shorter Poems (Faber).

For poems by George Barker, to the author and Faber & Faber Ltd.
Eros in Dogma (Faber).
Collected Poems, 1930–55 (Faber).
The True Confession of George Barker (Fore Publications).

For poems by William Bell, to Dr. H. C. Bell and Faber & Faber Ltd.
Mountains Beneath the Horizon (Faber).

For poems by John Betjeman, to the author and John Murray Ltd.
Selected Poems (John Murray).

For the poem by Laurence Binyon, to The Society of Authors.
The Purgatorio of Dante (Macmillan).

For the poem by Thomas Blackburn, to the author and The Hand and Flower Press.
The Outer Darkness (Hand and Flower Press).

For poems by Edmund Blunden, to the author and A. D. Peters.
Poems, 1914–1930 (Cobden-Sanderson).

For the poem by Wilfrid Scawen Blunt, to the Syndics of the Fitzwilliam Museum, Cambridge.
Poetical Works (Macmillan).

For poems by Robert Bridges, to The Clarendon Press, Oxford.
The Poetical Works of Robert Bridges (Clarendon Press).

For the poem by Rupert Brooke, to Sidgwick & Jackson Ltd.
Rupert Brooke: The Complete Poems (Sidgwick & Jackson).

For poems by Norman Cameron, to his literary executors.
Forgive Me Sire (Fore Publications).

For poems by Roy Campbell, to his literary executors and The Bodley Head Ltd.
Collected Poems (Bodley Head).

For the poem by Maurice Carpenter, to the author and The Phoenix Press.
IX Poems (Phoenix Press).

For the poem by Charles Causley, to the author and The Hand and Flower Press.
Farewell, Aggie Weston (Hand and Flower Press).

For poems by G. K. Chesterton, to Miss D. E. Collins, A. P. Watt & Son, Methuen & Co. Ltd. and J. M. Dent & Sons Ltd.

| *Collected Poems* (Methuen) | (*An Old Song*). |
| *The Wild Knight* (Dent) | (*The Skeleton*). |

For the poem by Jack Clemo, to the author and Methuen and Co. Ltd.
The Map of Clay (Methuen).

For the poem by A. E. Coppard, to his literary executors and A. D. Peters.
Collected Poems (Cape).

For the poem by Anthony Cronin, to the author and The Cresset Press, Ltd.
Poems (Cresset Press).

For the poem by John Davidson, to The Bodley Head Ltd.
Ballads and Songs (Bodley Head).

For the poem by Donald Davie, to the author.
Brides of Reason (Fantasy Press).

For poems by W. H. Davies, to Mrs. H. M. Davies and Jonathan Cape Ltd.
Complete Poems (Cape).

For poems by Walter de la Mare, to the Literary Trustees of Walter de la Mare and Faber & Faber Ltd.
Collected Poems (Faber).

For poems by C. M. Doughty, to the Executors of the late C. M. Doughty and the publishers Gerald Duckworth & Co. Ltd.
The Dawn in Britain (Cape).

For poems by Keith Douglas, to Editions Poetry London (Mandeville Publications).
Collected Poems (Editions Poetry London).
Selected Poems (Faber).

For the poem by Lawrence Durrell, to the author and Faber & Faber Ltd.
Collected Poems (Faber).

For poems by T. S. Eliot, to the author and Faber & Faber Ltd.
Collected Poems, 1909–1962 (Faber).

For poems by William Empson, to the author and Chatto and Windus Ltd.
Collected Poems (Chatto & Windus).

For the poem by Anne Finch, to the author and Sidgwick and Jackson Ltd.
Essay on Marriage (Sidgwick and Jackson).

For poems by James Elroy Flecker, to Martin Secker & Warburg Ltd.
Collected Poems (Secker & Warburg).

For poems by David Gascoyne, to the author, J. M. Dent & Sons Ltd. and John Lehmann Ltd.
Hölderlin's Madness (Dent).
Poems, 1937–1941 (Editions Poetry London).
A Vagrant (John Lehmann).

For the poem by Wilfred Gibson, to his literary executors and Macmillan & Co. Ltd.
Collected Poems (Macmillan).

For poems by W. S. Graham, to the author, Editions Poetry London (Mandeville Publications) and Faber & Faber Ltd.
2nd Poems (Editions Poetry London).
The White Threshold (Faber).

For poems by Robert Graves, to the author, A. P. Watt & Son and Cassell & Co Ltd.
Collected Poems, 1914–1947 (Cassell).

For the poem by Thom Gunn, to the author and Faber & Faber Ltd.
Fighting Terms (Faber).

For poems by Thomas Hardy, to the Trustees of the Hardy Estate and Macmillan & Co. Ltd.
Collected Poems (Macmillan).

For poems by Thomas Hennell, to Miss Betty Hennell and Oxford University Press.
Poems (O.U.P.).

For the poem by Rayner Heppenstall, to the author and Martin Secker & Warburg Ltd.
Poems, 1933–1945 (Secker & Warburg).

For poems by Brian Higgins, to the author and Longmans, Green & Co Ltd.
Notes While Travelling (Longmans).
'The Enticements of Virtue' and
'All Other Men' have not previously been
printed in book form.

For poems by Geoffrey Hill, to the author and André Deutsch Ltd.
For the Unfallen (Deutsch).

For poems by Ralph Hodgson, to Mrs. Hodgson and Macmillan & Co. Ltd.
Collected Poems (Macmillan).

For poems by A. E. Housman, to The Society of Authors as the literary representative of the A. E. Housman Estate and Jonathan Cape Ltd.
Collected Poems (Cape).

For the poem by Ted Hughes, to the author
'The Lake' has not previously been printed in book form.
For the extract from the poem by David Jones, to the author and Faber & Faber Ltd.
> *The Anathemata* (Faber).

For the poem by James Joyce, to the Trustees of the James Joyce Estate and Jonathan Cape Ltd.
> *The Essential James Joyce* (Cape).

For poems by Patrick Kavanagh, to the author and MacGibbon & Kee Ltd.
> *Collected Poems* (MacGibbon & Kee).

For poems by Sidney Keyes, to Routledge and Kegan Paul Ltd.
> *Collected Poems* (Routledge).

For poems by Rudyard Kipling, to Mrs. George Bambridge, A. P. Watt & Son, Methuen & Co. Ltd., Macmillan & Co. Ltd. and The Macmillan Co. of Canada.
> *Barrack Room Ballads* (Methuen).
> *Rewards and Fairies* (Macmillan).
> *The Five Nations* (Methuen).

For the poem by James Kirkup, to the author and Oxford University Press.
> *A Correct Compassion* (O.U.P.).

For the poem by Philip Larkin, to the author and Faber & Faber Ltd.
> *The Whitsun Weddings* (Faber).

For the poem by D. H. Lawrence, to the estate of Mrs. Frieda Lawrence and Laurence Pollinger Ltd.
> *Complete Poems* (Heinemann).

For the poem by Laurie Lee, to the author and The Hogarth Press Ltd.
> *The Sun My Monument* (Hogarth Press).

For the poem by Alun Lewis, to George Allen & Unwin Ltd.
> *Raider's Dawn* (Allen & Unwin).

For poems by C. Day Lewis, to the author and The Hogarth Press Ltd.
> *Collected Poems, 1929–1936* (Hogarth Press).

For the poem by Wyndham Lewis, to his literary executors and Methuen & Co. Ltd.
One Way Song (Methuen).

For poems by Malcolm Lowry, to his literary executors and City Lights Press, San Francisco.
Selected Poems (City Lights Press).

For poems by Hugh MacDiarmid, to the author, Macmillan & Co. Ltd., The Macmillan Co., New York and William MacLellan Publisher.
Selected Poems (Macmillan).
Selected Poems (MacLellan).
Collected Poems (Macmillan, N.Y.).

For the poem by Patrick Macdonogh, to the author.
Over the Water (Orwell Press).

For poems by Louis MacNeice, to Mrs. MacNeice and Faber & Faber Ltd.
Collected Poems (Faber).
The Burning Perch (Faber).

For the poem by John Masefield, to the author (Dr. John Masefield, O.M.) and The Society of Authors.
Collected Poems (Heinemann).

For poems by Harold Monro, to his literary executors.
Collected Poems (Cobden-Sanderson).

For the poem by T. Sturge Moore, to his literary executors and Macmillan & Co. Ltd.
The Poems of T. Sturge Moore (Macmillan).

For poems by Edwin Muir, to Mrs. Muir and Faber & Faber Ltd.
Collected Poems (Faber).

For the poem by Richard Murphy, to the author and Faber & Faber Ltd.
Sailing to an Island (Faber).

For poems by Sir Henry Newbolt, to the Executors of the late Sir Henry Newbolt, A. P. Watt & Son and John Murray Ltd.

Poems New and Old (Murray).

For the poem by Robert Nichols, to Mr. Milton Waldman and Wm. Collins and Co. Ltd.
Such Was My Singing (Collins).

For poems by Norman Nicholson, to the author and Faber & Faber Ltd.
Five Rivers (Faber).
Rock Face (Faber).

For poems by Wilfred Owen, to Chatto & Windus Ltd.
The Poems of Wilfred Owen (Chatto & Windus).

For poems by Herbert Palmer, to his literary executors, J. M. Dent & Sons Ltd. and George G. Harrap & Co. Ltd.
Collected Poems 1918–1931 (Dent)
A Sword in the Desert (Harrap) (*The Wounded Hawk*).

For poems by Ruth Pitter, to the author and The Cresset Press Ltd.
The Bridge (Cresset Press).
The Spirit Watches (Cresset Press).
A Trophy of Arms (Cresset Press).

For the poem by William Plomer, to the author and Jonathan Cape Ltd.
The Dorking Thigh (Cape).

For poems by Paul Potts, to the author and Editions Poetry London (Mandeville Publications).
Instead of a Sonnet (Editions Poetry London).

For poems by Ezra Pound, to Mrs. Dorothy Pound.
Personae (Faber).
The Pisan Cantos (Faber).

For the poem by F. T. Prince, to the author and Faber & Faber Ltd.
Poems (Faber).

For the poem by Kathleen Raine, to the author and Hamish Hamilton Ltd.
The Pythoness (Hamish Hamilton).

For poems by Sir Herbert Read, to the author and Faber & Faber Ltd.
Collected Poems (Faber).

For poems by Edgell Rickword, to the author and The Bodley Head Ltd.
Collected Poems (Bodley Head).

For poems by Anne Ridler, to the author and Faber & Faber Ltd.
The Nine Bright Shiners (Faber).

For poems by W. R. Rodgers, to the author and Martin Secker & Warburg Ltd.
>   *Awake!* (Secker & Warburg).
>   *Europa and the Bull* (Secker & Warburg).

For poems by Isaac Rosenberg, to Chatto & Windus Ltd.
>   *Collected Poems* (Chatto & Windus).

For poems by Siegfried Sassoon, to the author.
>   *Collected Poems* (Faber).

For the poem by Martin Seymour-Smith, to the author and Abelard-Schuman Ltd.
>   *Tea with Miss Stockport* (Abelard-Schuman).

For the poem by John Short, to the author and J. M. Dent & Sons Ltd.
>   *The Oak and the Ash* (Dent).

For poems by C. H. Sisson, to the author and Abelard-Schuman Ltd.
>   *The London Zoo* (Abelard-Schuman).
>   'The Nature of Man' and 'Adam and Eve' have not previously been printed in book form.

For poems by Dr. Edith Sitwell, to the author, David Higham Associates Ltd. and Macmillan & Co. Ltd.
>   *Collected Poems* (Macmillan).

For poems by Stevie Smith, to the author and Chapman & Hall Ltd.
>   *A Good Time Was Had By All* (Cape).
>   *Harold's Leap* (Chapman & Hall).
>   *Mother, What Is Man?* (Cape).

For the poem by Sydney Goodsir Smith, to the author.
>   *The Deevil's Waltz* (MacLellan).

For the poem by Bernard Spencer, to his literary executors and Hodder & Stoughton Ltd.
>   *With Luck Lasting* (Hodder & Stoughton).

For poems by Stephen Spender, to the author and Faber & Faber Ltd.
>   *Collected Poems* (Faber).

For the poem by J. C. Squire, to his literary executors.
Selected Poems (Macmillan).

For poems by Arthur Symons, to his literary executors and William Heineman Ltd.
Poems (Heinemann).

For poems by Dylan Thomas, to his literary executors and J. M. Dent & Sons Ltd.
Collected Poems (Dent).

For poems by Edward Thomas, to Mrs. Helen Thomas.
Collected Poems (Faber).

For the poem by R. S. Thomas, to the author and Rupert Hart-Davis Ltd.
Tares (Hart-Davis).

For the poem by Terence Tiller, to the author and The Hogarth Press, Ltd.
Reading a Medal (Hogarth Press).

For the poem by Charles Tomlinson, to the author and Oxford University Press.
A Peopled Landscape (O.U.P.).

For the poem by W. J. Turner, to his literary executors.
Fossils of a Future Time? (O.U.P.).

For poems by Vernon Watkins, to the author and Faber & Faber Ltd.
Ballad of the Mari Lwyd (Faber).
The Lady with the Unicorn (Faber).
Cypress and Acacia (Faber).

For the poem by Dorothy Wellesley, to her literary executors.
Selected Poems (Williams & Norgate).

For poems by Anna Wickham, to her literary executors.
The Man with a Hammer (Grant Richards).
The Little Old House (Poetry Bookshop).
The Contemplative Quarry (Poetry Bookshop).

For poems by Charles Williams, to Mrs. Williams and Oxford University Press.
Taliessin Through Logres (O.U.P.).
Poems of Conformity (O.U.P.).

For poems by W. B. Yeats, to Mrs. Yeats, A. P. Watt & Son and Macmillan & Co. Ltd.

Collected Poems of W. B. Yeats (Macmillan).

For poems by Andrew Young, to the author and Jonathan Cape Ltd.

The Collected Poems of Andrew Young (Cape).

INDEX OF FIRST LINES

Abelard was: God is	265
Above me the abbey, grey arches on the cliff,	239
A bush was on that dump:	101
After hot loveless nights, when cold winds stream	88
Again let me do a lot of extraordinary talking.	208
'Age, age,' groaned the hour-old midge	169
Alas! for all the pretty women who marry dull men,	334
Alex, perhaps a colour of which neither of us had dreamt	37
A livid sky on London	98
All day my sheep have mingled with yours	87
All last night I had quiet	36
All other men cower within their deeds	165
A lot of the old folk here—all that's left	217
Already, through the splendour ere the morn,	71
Amid the thunders of the falling Dark	289
Apollo kept my father's sheep,	227
A rosy shield upon its back,	348
Ash on an old man's sleeve	125
As I walked down by the river	96
As lambs into the pen of sheep	326
A song in the valley of Nemea:	123
A spirit seems to pass,	154
As the clouds that are so light,	317
At Dirty Dick's and Sloppy Joe's	43
Auden, MacNeice, Day Lewis, I have read them all,	217
Barefoot I went and made no sound;	249
Before I knocked and flesh let enter,	312
Being set on the idea	48
Beloved, may your sleep be sound	340
Beneath their flames, cities of candelabra	324
Bent double, like old beggars under sacks,	244
Better disguised than the leaf-insect,	175
But for lust we could be friends	250
Camões, alone, of all the lyric race	91
Carry her over the water	43

Chattering finch and water-fly	100
Chilled with salt dew, tossed on dark waters deep,	160
Christmas declares the glory of the flesh:	271
Cleanly, sir, you went to the core of the matter	194
Closed like confessionals, they thread	198
Cosmic Leviathan, that monstrous fish	269
Count up those books whose pages you have read	328
Cranmer was parson of this parish	284
Curtains of rock	138
Damn it all! all this our South stinks peace.	258
Dear, I must be gone	341
Deep in the fading leaves of light,	273
Downhill I came, hungry and yet not starved:	319
Down, wanton, down! Have you no shame	150
Dust thou Art, but dust carefully	170
Dying sun, shine warm a little longer!	152
Early sun on Beaulieu water	69
Ears in the turrets hear	315
Earth, receive an honoured guest;	46
First: The protracted fever	165
First the artillery groaned beyond the Channel	39
Friend, whose unnatural early death	136
From one shaft at Cleator Moor	237
From prehistoric distance, beyond clocks,	225
From the very first coming down	42
From what proud star I know not, but I found	76
Gently I wave the visible world away	310
Goneys an' gullies an' all o' the birds o' the sea	224
Had there been peace there never had been riven	39
Happy are men who yet before they are killed	241
Ha! sir, I have seen you sniffing and snoozling about among my flowers	260
Having written several poems which I will not publish	164
He came to visit me, my mortal messenger.	281

He planked down sixpence and he took his drink;	141
Her cheeks were white, her eyes were wild,	111
Here at the wayside station, as many a morning,	229
Her strong enchantments failing,	173
He strides across the grassy corn	347
He was a reprobate I grant	121
High the vanes of Shrewsbury gleam	173
His shadow monstrous on the palace wall,	73
Hours before dawn we were woken by the quake	130
I am the ghost of Shadwell Stair	241
I could not look on Death	193
I couldn't touch a stop and turn a screw	106
I'd been on duty from two till four	277
I encountered the crowd returning from amusements,	52
If any question why we died	192
I have been young, and now am not too old,	74
I have heard that hysterical women say	345
I have with fishing-rod and line	245
I killed them, but they would not die	275
I look into my glass	158
I looked into my heart to write	55
I love my little son, and yet when he was ill	215
I may be smelly and I may be old,	295
I met ayont the cairney	216
In a garden shady this holy lady	44
In a solitude of the sea	157
In his tall senatorial	286
I never look upon the sea	246
In our town people live in rows	333
In the first year of the last disgrace	57
In the gloom of whiteness,	319
In the smoky outhouses of the court of love	86
In this house, she said, in this high second storey	308
In valleys green and still	171
I sat by the granite pillar, and sunlight fell	233
I saw a staring virgin stand	344
I saw a vulture in the sky	325
I saw old Duchesses with their young loves,	335
I sent a letter to my love	51
I sigh for the heavenly country	298

I sought a theme and sought for it in vain,	343
I stoop to gather a seabird's feather	327
I think a time will come when you will understand	254
I thought I was so tough,	153
It is the nature of man that puzzles me	283
'I was a Have.' 'I was a "Have-not".'	193
I was of delicate mind. I stepped aside for my needs.	193
I wish there were a touch of these boats about my life;	302
I wonder poet, can you take it	254
I would that folk forgot me quite,	155
Just a line to remind my friends that after much trouble	184
Kabul town's by Kabul river,	188
Leafy-with-love banks and the green waters of the canal	181
Leave Helen to her lover. Draw away	265
Let her lie naked here, my hand resting	58
Like a lizard in the sun, though not scuttling	149
Like the first seed before man's birth,	34
Listen. Put on morning,	145
Living in a wide landscape are the flowers—	121
Local I'll bright my tale on, how	143
Lovers may find similitudes	269
Love that drained her drained him she'd loved, though each	167
Maidens who this bursting May	61
Marston, dropping it in the grate, broke his pipe	305
May I for my own self song's truth reckon,	255
Mazing around my mind like moths at a shaded candle	81
More beautiful than any gift you gave	263
More kicks than pence	183
Most lovely Dark, my Aethiopia born	292
'Music for a while'	238
My black hills have never seen the sun rising,	181
Myself unto myself will give	178
Nature that day a woman was in weakness,	78
Nearing again the legendary isle	206
Never presume that in this marble stable	40

Note this survivor, bearing the mark of the violator,	331
Now it is autumn and the falling fruit	199
Now Philippa is gone, that so divinely	272
Now she is like the white tree-rose	207
Now stoops the sun, and dies day's cheerful light	119
O for our upland meads,	159
O, have you seen the leper healed,	330
Oh who is that young sinner with the handcuffs on his wrists?	172
O, love, in your sweet name enough	132
O Merlin in your crystal cave	231
Once on a time I used to be	235
On the first hour of my first day	193
On windy days the mill	103
O, she walked unaware of her own increasing beauty	220
O Son of mine, when dusk shall find thee bending	233
Over rock and wrinkled ground	273
Over the land freckled with snow half-thawed	320
O wha's been here afore me, lass,	215
Phoenix, bird of terrible pride,	267
Phyllidula is scrawny but amorous	260
Poor Doctor Blow went out of church	159
Queen Bess was Harry's daughter. Stand forward, partners all!	190
Red fool, my laughing comrade;	205
Rin and rout, rin and rout,	299
Ripeness is all; her in her cooling planet	129
Rumbling under blackened girders, Midland, bound for Cricklewood	67
Said the Lion to the Lioness—'When you are amber dust,—	288
Sempronius,	119
Shall I write pretty poetry	333
She flourished in the 'Twenties, hectic days of Peace,	251
She grew ninety years through sombre winter,	228

She tells her love while half-asleep,	150
She turned in the high pew, until her sight	154
Ship's master:	176
Shouldering shapes of the skies of Broceliande	338
Silent is Orpheus now, and silent now	62
Since I have seen a bird one day	111
Sith, in dark speech, Carvilios hymn unfolds,	118
Slowly the daylight left our listening faces	279
Sprawled on the bags and crates in the rear of the truck	84
Stand on the highest pavement of the stair—	124
Stay, spring, for by this ruthless haste	347
Strangely assorted, the shape of song and the bloody man	247
Stranger, you who hide my love	306
Strolling one afternoon along a street	278
Success is like some horrible disaster	214
Tall nettles cover up, as they have done	317
'Tell me, tell me,	114
That civilization may not sink,	340
The barrack-square, washed clean with rain,	277
The conductor's hands were black with money:	222
The day that *Youth* had died	82
The few syllables of a horse's scuffle at the edge of the road	283
The fire was furry as a bear	286
The Firm of Happiness, Limited, was one to astonish the stars	85
The flowers that in thy garden rise,	232
The full moon easterly rising, furious;	148
The Garden called Gethsemane	192
The gean trees drive me to love	146
The girl's far treble, muted to the heat,	204
The gold-armoured ghost from the Roman road	293
The great cup tumbled, ringing like a bell	187
The grey wolf comes again: I had made fast	311
The hop-poles stand in cones,	74
The House is crammed: tier beyond tier they grin	278
The hunchback in the park	313
The important thing is not	182
The King's poet was his captain of horse in the wars	336

The leaves looked in at the window	169
The modern malady of love is nerves	310
The monk sat in his den,	296
The Movement, she explained	170
The nearly right	297
The old professor of Zoology	134
The raging and the ravenous,	248
There's a brief spring in all of us and when it finishes	93
There was a Boy bedded in bracken	282
These errors loved no less than the saint loves arrows	56
The sun used to shine while we two walked	318
The swallow flew like lightning over the green	75
The tiger in the tiger-pit	125
The wood was rather old and dark	294
They, after the slow building of the house,	168
They must be shown as about to taste of the tree.	284
They named it Aultgraat—Ugly Burn,	348
They set the fish upon the table,	33
This bread I break was once the oat,	315
This legend is told of me	163
This mast, new-shaved, through whom I rive the ropes	89
Those Cambridge generations, Russell's, Keynes' ...	110
Toledo, when I saw you die	88
Tonight the moon is high, to summon all	64
Too long outside your door I have shivered	225
To speak in summer in a lecture hall	184
To the much-tossed Ulysses, never done	149
Tudor indeed is gone and every rose,	261
Unfriendly friendly universe,	230
Up the ash tree climbs the ivy,	68
Wan	295
Wearing worry about money like a hair shirt	264
We curl into your eyes—	275
We're going to the fair at Holstenwall,	186
What is the world, O soldiers?	115
What is this recompense you'd have from me?	86
What thou lovest well remains,	261
When I was born on Amman hill	328

When mountain rocks and leafy trees	151
When you and my true lover meet	342
Where has tenderness gone, he asked the mirror	214
While northward the hot sun was sinking o'er the trees	79
'Who are we waiting for?' '*Soup* burnt?'.... Eight—	115
'Who are you, Sea Lady,	133
Who goes there? God knows. I'm nobody. How should I answer?	81
Who, minter of medallions,	323
With a pert moustache and a ready candid smile	222
With the exact length and pace of his father's stride	105
Yes as alike as entirely	142
Yesterday I found one left:	321
You must have been still sleeping, your wife there	139
You never heard a snail in song?	169
Your body derns	216
Your body is stars whose million glitter here:	305